The Disney Difference

The Complete Guide to Adding Disney Magic to Your Organization

Wayne Olson

Theme Park Press
www.ThemeParkPress.com

Editor: Bob McLain
Layout: Artisanal Text

ISBN 978-1-68390-027-6
Printed in the United States of America

Theme Park Press | **www.ThemeParkPress.com**
Address queries to bob@themeparkpress.com

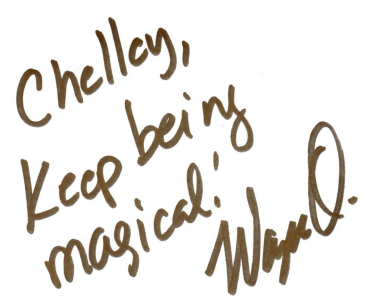

Chelley,
Keep being
magical!

Wyn O.

For Heather, Nathan and Mark

Contents

Foreword by Lee Cockerell vii

Introduction ix

1 The Magic of Walt Disney 1

2 Widen Your World 29

3 First Impressions Last 49

4 Once Upon a Dream 75

5 The Personal Touch 97

6 We Work So Others Play 123

7 Believe 131

8 A Great Big Beautiful Tomorrow 155

Afterword by Bob Gurr 167

Selected Bibliography 169

About the Author 173

More Books from Theme Park Press 175

Praise for
The Disney Difference

"I've read lots of books about Disney, and this one is a gem. Read it for new insights and useful ideas."

—Mark Sanborn, Author of *The Fred Factor*

"*The Disney Difference* is packed with enjoyable history about Walt Disney and his 'world.' But more than a fun Disney archive, Wayne Olson's book emphasizes the importance of customer relations through the Disney lens. That's why I recommend it. Dazzling customers with remarkable service. Yes!"

—Dan T. Cathy, Chairman and CEO of Chick-fil-A

"This is a wonderful book. It's not only a tribute to Walt Disney and the philosophy that helped make Disneyland the showcase for an entire industry, but it details that philosophy beautifully and outlines how it can be applied to every business endeavor, large or small. Whatever Walt did he did from his heart. To see the things he believed in being interpreted and incorporated in so many areas of business would make him very proud. It is a must-read!"

—Rolly Crump, Disney Imagineer

"Executives who strive for improvement look to the handful of organizations that excel decade after decade. Disney is one of these. Wayne Olson has done a masterful job of identifying the service-centric culture that is inherent to Disney's success. Whether you have customers, patients, donors, or constituents, I heartily recommend this book."

—Ron Klein, Inc. 500 Entrepreneur

"Wayne Olson has written a manual on how to move any organization from good to great to greater. This book will help anyone in any organization to be a better manager and leader. Walt Disney was a master at attention to detail and was a great leader as well. Don't read this book, study it and implement what you learn and your organization will create magic, too, in customer service and in bottom line results."

—Lee Cockerell, Former Executive Vice President Walt Disney World Resort, Author of *Creating Magic*, *Time Management Magic*, *The Customer Rules*, and *Career Magic*

"As the Founder of Famous Dave's of America and winner of over 750 Best of Class awards, I eagerly devoured the insights of Wayne's book, *The Disney Difference*. Wayne spills the beans on the Secret Sauce that has created Disney's 'special magic' that has made the Disney brand Best of Class both stateside and globally. You can only make this happen when you focus on building great people both in your business and in your community. I urge you to get this book NOW!"

—Famous Dave Anderson, America's Rib King and Founder, Famous Dave's of America, Inc.

"Having spent an entire career in the theme park industry, I have always used Walt's way to inspire staff, from front line to senior leadership. Walt was one of my mentors and I have always loved his attention to detail and exceeding the guest expectations. Wayne's book captures the true spirit of the Disney way and I will use the book as a guide for my team."

—Thom Stork, President and CEO, The Florida Aquarium

"After building homes in Disney's new town, Celebration, for more than 20 years, and learning the 'Disney Way,' I found this book captures the magic of creating a unique customer and donor experience!"

—David Weekley, Founder David Weekley Homes

"A compelling story of relentless customer focus and incredible attention to detail that has set Disney apart from all others. It provides a roadmap on how to deliver the elevated customer experience."

—C. Richard Weylman, CSP, CPAE, Author of *The Power of Why—Breaking Out in a Competitive Marketplace*

"Wayne Olson has put 20 lbs of bbq in a 1 lb cup. The difference with *The Disney Difference* is that Wayne has succinctly tapped into the soul of the Disney success. With astute business insights and practical everyday applications, he has made a direct connection with my heart and mind. I am now filled with ideas for new ways to grow and build our business AND our people. Every restaurant owner needs to read this book...really!"

—Jim H. Kelley, Co-owner Lawlers Barbecue

"Wayne reminds us through the 'Disney Way' that it takes people to make our dreams come true. What a wonderful message for team members and managers that may lose customer focus at times. Wayne's book reinforces us to hold our Customer Covenant close to heart."

—Michael E. Hardin, Executive Vice-President,
Synovus Trust Company, N.A.

"Having retired after 21 years at Walt Disney World, meeting Wayne Olson has become one of my best takeaways. His sincere love of Disney shines brightly through the pages of his book."

—Dean Gaschler, Retired Disney Cast Member

"Not like other books that explore the magic of the Disney way, *The Disney Difference* is different itself. Using a delightful and engaging writing style, Wayne Olson dives deep into the many principles on which Walt Disney founded his empire, and clearly illustrates how we can apply them to our businesses, our volunteer interests, and our lives. Corporate leaders and nonprofit fundraisers alike can learn so much from the simple and practical lessons that are on every page of *The Disney Difference*."

—Richard Hadden, Co-author,
Contented Cows Still Give Better Milk

"Wayne in this practical book has dissected the Walt Disney business model into a 'how-to-do-it' valuable treatise for any business or profession. A must-read for new or old practitioners."

—Jerry Summers, Esq., Author of *Rush to Judgment*,
Partner, Summers, Rufolo and Rodgers

"Wayne has captured the most compelling components of the Disney difference in this easy-to-read and easy-to-apply book on Walt's customer-centered commitment to excellence, innovation, and of course, that magical experience."

—R Dr. William S. Barnes, Former Lead Pastor, St. Luke's United Methodist Church, Windermere, Florida

"Anytime you can look behind the curtain of Disney to see what makes them tick, you are equipped with special insight. Wayne Olson proves to be a skilled guide into the magic that can be transferable for any enterprise that combines people and money in his book *The Disney Difference.*"

—Larry Kreider, The Gathering/USA
Director of Partnerships

"As an Orlando resident, I can say there is definitely something magical about Walt Disney World. Just spend five minutes there and even the parking is a pleasant experience. Wayne Olson has picked and mined his way through Walt Disney history to provide readers with dozens of take-aways to turn their own business into a magical experience. Wayne does an excellent job illustrating his points with real-life stories about the Disney Way showing that these principles work in real-life, so why not at your business, too."

—Troy Schmidt, Author & Television Writer

"In my profession, superb customer service defines our yesterday, today, and tomorrow. In this must-read for all business owners, Wayne masterfully identifies how Walt Disney took customer service to an unprecedented level, casting a platinum standard for centuries to come."

—Charles "Chuck" Rice, Chick-fil-A Owner/ Operator, Retired Air Force Colonel

"I spent over 30 years in the theme park industry in senior management positions at Busch Gardens Tampa and SeaWorld of Florida. During this time, I developed an enormous respect for Disney and the way they operated. After retirement, I was so impressed with Disney that I decided to work at Disney World as a seasonal employee to get a closer look. The first day at Disney orientation I felt "pixie dust" settling on my head. I only worked there for four months and it was quite an entertaining experience. Everything that I imagined about Disney was verified. The employees were excellent, all aspects of the park were sparkling clean, and the time management of their staff was a productivity wonder. Wayne's book is an efficient guide for companies to follow in order to start getting their own pixie dust spread throughout their organization."

—Fred Peacock, Vice President of Operations for Busch Gardens Tampa and Sea World Orlando

"It's all about change, because change is the one universal constant. The key is to lead the change in the right direction. Wayne Olson gets it. In his new book, *The Disney Difference*, he uses the lessons taught by Disney to help organizations create the very change they need. His book is beyond helpful, and even insightful. His work is truly transformational."

—Patrick J. Day, CEO, Patrick Henry Family Services

"In *The Disney Difference*, Wayne Olson does an awesome job of capturing the essence of the success of Disney. It can be summed up in one word: culture. As the lead pastor of a church in the Orlando area, with a campus that shares a lake with Walt Disney World, I could resonate with Wayne's words on what makes Disney, Disney. Every day I live the 'Disney Difference' with everyone from executives at Disney to housekeepers in their world-class hotels. Walt Disney didn't create a new business model, he created a new culture. Guest experience, excellence, innovation, and personnel training were essential in getting it right; it's all part of the Disney culture. Wayne has done an excellent job of bringing out those transferable truths that can benefit any business. *The Disney Difference* is a must-read for those who want their organization to maximize its potential."

—Dr. Chuck Carter, Lead Pastor, First Baptist Church, Windermere, Florida

Foreword

Wayne Olson's new book gives us many great pointers and ideas on how following Walt Disney's philosophy on total and complete attention to detail can help you create magic in your organization. On page 10 we learn an important lesson about bumping the lamp which is an excellent example of "everything matters."

From the simplest things like listening intently to your customers and employees you will learn vital information you can implement in your own organization.

You will learn how vital the basics and common sense approaches are, including serious attention to cleanliness and friendliness, and how they separated Disney from everyone else in the world, and still do today.

Walt knew what we all should know by now, that you must hire the best team you can and make sure you are giving them the training, development, appreciation, recognition, and encouragement they deserve so they can perform their role in the show and be inspired to stay with the company.

This book is about how the real magic is created at Disney, and it all started with Walt.

You will learn how Walt's imagination, engagement, persistence, risk taking, and an unbelievable can-do attitude formed the foundation for the continued growth of one of the greatest companies in the world.

You will learn the reasons why Walt was so insistent on calling customers "guests," employees "cast members," and the workplace "on stage" and "backstage."

If you have always wanted to learn how Disney performs way beyond the expectations of their guests, then you will love this book. Not only will you love it but you will learn many concepts and philosophies you can apply today, no matter the size of your company or what it does.

You will learn about the names on the windows on Main Street, U.S.A., and why they are there.

You will learn how Walt applied all five senses to his work, including sight, smell, taste, feel, and hearing, to create the Disney Difference. He even applied the sixth sense, a sense of humor, to round it all out.

I ran Disney World operations for ten years and I thought I knew just about everything, but I learned lots of new information reading this book that I wish I had known when I joined Disney.

Every day around the world the big red curtain opens at Disney theme parks to start another performance like no other in the world. Disney parks are places where fantasy is real and reality is fantastic. The Disney Difference is real. Study this book and learn how you can create magic in your organization.

As Walt said, "If you can dream it, you can do it," and Walt did it by adding The Disney Difference to everything he did. Enjoy the journey.

— Lee Cockerell, Executive Vice President, Operations (Retired and Inspired), Walt Disney World Resort, Author of *Creating Magic*, *The Customer Rules*, *Time Management Magic*, and *Career Magic*

Introduction

Makes a Difference Who You Are

Your decision to invest your time and perhaps a few dollars in this book reveals something important about you. You care about those you serve. You also want to do a better job for the corporation, organization, educational institution, or charity you represent. You want to grow, and you want to know how learning about Walt Disney will help you do that.

However, there is something else about you that you might not have considered. This book's mission is to recognize and develop this notion and grow it within you. What is this notion? It's simple.

You matter.

No one can do your job like you can do your job. How you answer the phone, how you interact with others, and the smile on your face are as individual as your fingerprints. While we can always do our jobs better, no one can do your job like you can. And while we can all improve ourselves by adding skills, experience, and training, all of that is learned in the context of, and through the prism of, our personalities.

Walt Disney was quick to appreciate the importance of the individual. Each person was unique, and Walt was careful who he hired. He knew you could not separate a person from that person's skills and abilities. The "who" of the person he hired was as important as what that person knew. Perhaps even more importantly, he emphasized the need to treat each customer and guest as the individuals they were.

We can all benefit by looking at ourselves and our jobs the way Walt Disney did. He wanted to please his customers (his guests), and he hired the right people to make that happen. He understood that people are much more than a collection of talent and experience. People are a total package, and who you hire to deliver the service or make the goods is as important as the service or the goods themselves.

If you work for a nonprofit organization, or in a for-profit corporation where you are in contact with others, who you are matters. It's all about you. Your personality. Your outlook. Your approach. It all matters.

In every sales, customer service, or fundraising position, who you are is important. In many cases, who you are matters as much or more than what you know. Even for those of us who have no direct contact with customers or the public, we can still use the examples from Walt Disney in the way we treat fellow employees, supervisors, and managers.

Walt Disney recognized this basic principle. Everything he dreamed, designed, and did was focused on the individual. He was relentless in developing talent among those who worked for him and with him, and was no less persistent in insisting his audience was not a group or crowd as much as it was a collection of individuals, each with his or her own personality, desires, dreams, and wishes.

Unfortunately, we live in a world that while claiming to be more personal and connected is actually increasingly impersonal, if not overwhelmingly cold. Countless calls are answered by machine. "Press one" is usually the first thing we hear when calling just about anyone. People are so used to texting,

> "You can dream, create, design and build the most wonderful place in the world, but it takes people to make the dream a reality."
>
> — Walt Disney

many are concerned we are losing even the basic skills to communicate effectively with one another.

Companies, organizations, and even friends are becoming more distant. Even during his time, Walt Disney was trying to bring people together. He realized people were becoming separated from one another, and it was important to bring them closer.

Today, text messages have replaced phone calls. Emailed messages have replaced conversations. While technology is wonderful and is responsible for many advances, it can never replace human contact. When we lose touch with our customers, donors, and prospects, we lose business. We lose friends. We lose customers. Unfortunately, as a nation we are losing touch, and as a result, service satisfaction is at an all-time low.

> "Service in this country is so bad; you can offer above-average customer service and still stink... Ignore your industry's benchmarks and copy Disney's."
>
> —Harry Beckwith

However, it does not have to be that way. If we try to harness some of Walt Disney's principles, we can excel beyond our wildest dreams. In a world that expects disappointment or poor service, our attempts to connect with those we serve will be noticed and appreciated. Our work is worth it.

Small Efforts Big Rewards

Walt Disney knew the difference between success and failure was not a long journey—in either direction. You can move from ordinary to extraordinary with just a few small steps. Your smile can change an everyday experience to a pleasant one for your customer. Your helping hand can transform a one-time visitor to a life-long customer.

You make the difference.

You are the difference.

Remember, as you read these pages, who you are matters. The great thing is that no matter how many people read this book, each can find significance and greatness, because each will accomplish it in his or her own way.

At first it might seem Walt Disney's approach would not work for any non-artistic endeavor. How does a theme park relate to the administration of a military contractor? How does making an animated movie relate to the running of a factory? The answer lies in how we approach our staff, our customers, and the product or service we make or offer.

No matter what we do, people look to us for the same reasons. They want us to make their lives better. Ultimately, whatever our product may be, people want us to do something that will bring comfort and happiness to their lives, or at least make their lives easier. Maybe without even realizing it, everyone we meet secretly desires to be better off after having met us. And even if they didn't, there is no harm in approaching them as if they did.

In the pages that follow we will explore how Walt Disney approached his movies, theme parks, and consumer products. We will look behind the scenes at how Walt and his company accomplished so much, on a surprisingly limited budget. We will learn how we can all relate to our customers, clients, charitable donors, and friends a little more like Disney. When we do, we will dazzle them and amaze ourselves with all we can accomplish. In the end, we and they should all be better than we were before.

CHAPTER ONE

The Magic of Walt Disney

One Man's Vision

Perhaps more than anyone in the 20th century, Walt Disney had an ability to connect with people. He and the company he built could make millions laugh, cry, cheer, and smile. His movies, products, and theme parks have entertained and educated countless people. Walt Disney knew, maybe better than anyone, what people wanted and he delivered it to them. As we follow Walt's example, no matter what our endeavor, we'll find more success in everything we do.

Few people have influenced our culture as much as Walt Disney. From Tampa to Tokyo, everyone knows the characters, corporation, and empire built by the master entertainer. Throughout his life and career, Walt redefined movies, music, and outdoor entertainment. No other icon is as instantly recognizable as is his most famous creation, Mickey Mouse.

During his life and for more than a half century since his death, Walt Disney has set standards in entertainment and in customer service that many corporations and organizations do their best to copy and follow; and for good reason. As we strive to improve profits for our company, or multiply donations to our nonprofit organizations, or simply do our jobs better, we can all benefit by doing everything a little more like Disney.

There really is no magic to the way Disney does things. At its core, Disney's success can be attributed to a simple idea: care for your customer. Everything else the company produces—the creativity, the innovation, the laughs, the smiles, the charm, and the fantasy—springs from a deep, heartfelt desire to deliver joy to all those who buy, use, or visit a Disney production.

My goal in this book is to explore how Walt approached his business, and teach how we can follow Walt's lead and employ some of his magic in our everyday lives and careers.

The Enduring Allure of Fantasy

Walt Disney had an amazingly profound effect on modern life. It's hard to live anywhere on this planet without being influenced, or at least see evidence of, Walt Disney's broad appeal. Yet, while many of us see Disney's creations in some form every day, few of us take time to peek backstage to see how it all works. If we can employ just some of Disney's techniques, we can make a significant difference for our cause, our organization, and our careers.

Even if we have never been to a Disney park, seen a Disney movie,

While few of us would claim to be as creative as Walt Disney, we can learn from the phenomenal success that is Disney.

or purchased a Disney toy, the Disney influence has reached us. Walt Disney impacted not just his customers and his audience, but the entire globe. In a sense, Walt Disney re-wrote history even as he was creating a new history of his own.

King of the Child Frontier

For more than 150 years, school children and politicians alike marveled at the stories of the frontiersman David Crockett. Never during his life nor in any history book was he called "Davy," or "King of the Wild Frontier." He blazed trails throughout the south and the west as David, was elected to congress as David, and died at the Alamo as David. Yet in 1955, Walt Disney gave the historical figure known as David Crockett a new name: *Davy*.

From that year on, David Crockett, the historical figure, would become *Davy* Crockett and would look a lot more like the actor Fess Parker, whose appearance was nothing like the character he portrayed. Fess Parker was more than 9½ inches higher than David Crockett and bore no physical resemblance to the historical figure. Yet, when Walt Disney gave Crockett the informal name, Davy, and then cast the friendly and likeable Fess Parker as the historical figure, he changed Crockett lore forever. And

In the 1934 musical, *You're the Top*, and its title number, Cole Porter would write, "You're the top...you're Mickey Mouse." 20 years before Disneyland, Walt Disney and his mouse were already an American icon.

when he costumed Fess Parker for the role, he also transformed our children's imaginations. With the simple addition of an unusual hat to the character's outfit, children everywhere could pretend to be the frontiersman just by wearing a coonskin cap.

Prop Culture

The famous coonskin cap worn by Fess Parker was also a 20th century Disney addition to Crockett lore. David never wore one. However, to the dismay and detriment of raccoons everywhere, at the height of the Crockett craze in the 1950s, Disney sold more than 5,000 coonskin hats per day.

No one ever called Crockett "Davy" during his life, nor for decades after his death. Today, however, ask anyone the name of the frontiersman named Crockett who died at the Alamo, and the answer will always be "Davy," without the person ever realizing that Walt Disney had a role in shaping the response.

In the same way, if you have ever talked like a pirate by using words like "matey" or "arrghh," then you, too, have felt the Disney cultural impact. Before Robert Newton portrayed Long John Silver in Disney's *Treasure Island* (1950), no one knew what pirates sounded like. It took a Disney movie to teach us. Before Disney, pirates talked just like anyone else. Walt Disney gave our culture the sounds and language of pirates.

If you have ever heard an organ pound out "da da da da ta da...charge!" at a stadium event, then you have been touched by Disney. Although others claim to have written it, Disneyland entertainment director Thomas Walker is widely recognized as the author of the memorable charge for the USC Trojan Warriors that

Ever been to Disneyland? That was definitely an E-ticket."

— Astronaut Sally Ride describing the thrill of experiencing a space shuttle launch.

has been copied and repeated for decades.

If you take a child to a zoo or into the woods on a campout and he or she spots a deer, its name will inevitably be Bambi. An elephant is almost always Dumbo. Clownfish? Nemo. A lion is called Simba. The Disney influence spreads well beyond its immediate audience. Today, many names, themes, and ideas permeate our culture, all because of the vision of one man.

Just as Walt Disney shaped our culture, we can shape our organization. We can use some of the same strategies and enjoy some of the same groundbreaking results. Whether we work in a one-person start-up organization in a garage or have 5,000 employees reporting to us, we *can* all put a little Disney magic in everything we do. A little effort in one area can have ripples of excellence throughout our organizations and across those we serve.

Everything Matters

The problem with most businesses or organizations is they forget (or never learn) their priorities. They focus on one thing or another, but fail to recognize the singularly important concept that is the bedrock of the Disney way: *everything matters*.

Walt Disney understood that his guests (or audience or consumers) notice everything. From design to production to delivery to follow-through, there is nothing that does not count. The Disney way is evident and defined by everything the company does.

Everything Speaks

Walt Disney was fond of saying, "Everything speaks." Walt realized he was giving his customers a show, and every part of that show mattered. For the show to work, every element had to be considered. Every segment mattered. These two words, "everything speaks," capture the Disney philosophy and ethos more than any other words ever written by the company, or about the company, or about Walt Disney himself.

Consider "everything speaks" in terms of a cowboy movie. Even with a great script, talented direction, fantastic sets, thrilling stunts, and the most charismatic actors, it will not do well if the costuming department dresses everyone in 1950s milkman uniforms. It will become a comedy, whether it is intended to be or not.

What is our business? Whether we sell copying machines or raise money to cure cancer, everything matters. What if we are taking a big customer or wealthy donor to dinner? It is time for the big pitch. We have practiced our presentation, we have done our research, and we know the prospect is poised to act. We are one step away from closing the deal.

However, at the fine restaurant where we eat, we chew with our mouths open, talk over the prospect, or offend the wait staff. We may not ever realize we have offended the prospect, but we have. The experience we give our customers matters as much as the outcome. The journey defines the destination.

Even if we are selling wonderful copiers or are innovative with a new toothpaste formula, the prospect might have other options just as good, if not better. To dazzle, we must win the prospect on almost every level. A loss in one is often a loss in all. We may never know the impression we make, but the deal is sunk because we fail to appreciate what Walt embraced: *everything matters*.

A cake with the finest flour, creamiest milk, and silkiest frosting will taste horrible if the chef forgets to add eggs to the cake mix. In the same way, Walt realized every ingredient is important in everything we do. To have a great cake, all of the ingredients must be good and in proper portion, and not just a few or some of them.

We cannot count on our customers to see only the things we want them them to see or see them in the way we want them to see them. Rather, customers will choose what to see, and will choose how to see it. Our customers and donors determine what is important. The prospect is always in control. Rarely are we.

The best test of whether we have our audience or our customer in mind is a simple one. When we are choosing to do something and we make our decision by using the words "they won't mind" or "it'll be okay with him or her," then we have not given our best to the effort. When we excuse an action (or inaction) because we think it will be okay, then we have set up our customers and ourselves for disappointment. In the same way, if we choose to do something because we can get away with it, or no one will say anything, then we have likely not done ourselves any good.

Even if our product is the best on the market and offered at the fairest price, a customer may look elsewhere if we are late for the appointment, look sloppy, or use one coat of paint instead of two.

If we do not take the time to be on time, or look appropriate to the occasion, the prospect may overlook it. But maybe not. Maybe we feel being late is excusable, or dress is not important. We may think it's okay. But our thoughts are irrelevant. In Walt's world, everything speaks, and every part of our presentation matters, because our customers or donors evaluate them all.

When we cut corners or fail to do something because it will be okay if we don't, our results will be, at best, just okay. After all, that is the standard we have set for ourselves. If we give a mediocre effort, then we should expect the same outcome. If we decide we can end our efforts at some level where the customer will be "okay" with the results, then that is the feedback, and word-of-mouth we can expect to return to us. For example, if it is "okay" not to send a handwritten thank-you note to a customer or donor and we choose not to write one, we have made a non-Disney decision.

It's true the customer may indeed be just fine without the handwritten thank-you note, and likely will never complain about not receiving one. At the same time, that customer will not go out of his way to use us again, or worse, will not recommend us to others. It is only when we seek to meet customers where they are, and then do more, that we excel and receive the coveted repeated business and positive word-of-mouth we all want.

It is better to do a few things consistently well than many things poorly.

Don't Strip the Straps

Early in the life of Disneyland there was a stagecoach ride in Frontierland. You could board an authentic, beautifully restored 19th century coach behind a team of live horses. John Hench designed the attraction using modern rubber sheathes as shock absorbers instead of the layers of leather that would have been used a hundred years earlier. Hench reasoned, and rightly so, that the modern material would provide a better ride, would last longer, and would be less expensive and easier to maintain and replace. All true, plus one other important detail: guests will never see the elastic material. It is under the carriage and out of sight from anyone who is not an expert on that type of coach.

Walt Disney demanded that Hench replace the rubber with leather. Hench was confused. He had given Walt everything he requested. He designed a good attraction with a smooth ride, with readily available materials that were easily replaceable, inexpensive, and unnoticeable to the untrained eye.

Walt Disney explained that guests may not exactly notice what material was between them and the wheels, but they would *know*. Even without any idea what a true stagecoach would look or feel like, guests would somehow appreciate the dedication to authenticity. As Walt would say to attraction designer Hench, "They just know."

To be like Walt Disney, we can't have excellence in some areas and mediocrity in others. The excellent things we do will not pull up the average things we do. Rather, average work seems to have greater power to pull excellence down. People may notice excellence in some areas, but will spend their dollars elsewhere if the excellence is not spread evenly throughout the organization. Disney understood this and mastered it. So can we.

Show Them You Care

Just like Walt showed with his insistence on using leather straps, many attribute Walt's success, and today, all of the Disney company's accomplishments, to "attention to detail." While it's true you can find magnificence in the details of any Disney production, it is more than that. The details are important to Disney, but it is not truly all that matters. It is a dedication to giving your guests (or customer, donor, or audience) the best you can give. This means not just the things on the surface, but throughout. The details are the consistent result of the effort, not necessarily the goal.

"Attention to detail" is perhaps better described as commitment to integrity. Walt Disney wanted each of his products to have *integrity*—not necessarily the kind of integrity that evokes images of moral righteousness, though that is important as well. Disney's integrity relates to believability and an understanding by the creator and the consumer that all parts of the show fit together perfectly for a seamless product. Nothing is out of place. Like Hench's stagecoach, nothing is in the finished product that does not belong, and everything that would be in the product is present.

Bump the Lamp

Even after Walt's death, this commitment to integrity continues in the company today. In the 1988 movie

Who Framed Roger Rabbit, the detective character, played by Bob Hoskins, picks up Roger Rabbit and bumps Roger's head on an overhead lamp. The bump was not in the script, and is something that just happened during filming. Because it was unplanned, the director, animators, and editors had to decide how the swinging lamp would change the scene.

The rabbit character was animated, but Bob Hoskins and the setting were real. As the lamp swayed from side to side it cast a shadow over Hoskins and the real-life background. Animators drew Roger Rabbit, but they also drew the lamp's shadow over Roger Rabbit. If the character were really in the setting, the shadow would cast over him as well. Adding shadow to a character by hand is not as easy as drawing a shadow. As the shadow crossed over Roger, the color of his fur and clothing had to become subtly darker, then return to normal just as subtly when the shadow left. It was not adding a shadow as much as it was completely redrawing the character in every frame.

It took the animators more time and effort to add the shadow across Roger Rabbit. But for the scene to have integrity, adding the shadow was a must. The animators could have left out the shadow, and no one would likely have noticed, at least on the surface. Even more incredible is that few people would even notice the shadow once they added it. However, Walt would say, had he been involved in the production, that people may never notice the added detail, but they would somehow know everything seemed right. It held together. It worked. While commitment to integrity shows up in details, the details are the product, not the goal, of the Disney company's productions.

Walt Disney demanded attention to the customer at every step and with every decision. Even things in the background that the guest might never completely notice are important. People may see excellence but will not do business with us if greatness is limited to one or two areas of our organization. We must be committed to the total guest/donor/customer experience, and not just pushing one part here or there. Integrity is the key. Everything speaks.

Let the Show Begin

Disney has another secret related to integrity. The show does not begin when the curtain rises. It doesn't even begin when the audience member takes his or her seat. Think more broadly. It doesn't begin in the lobby, the sidewalk, or even the parking lot. The show begins when the audience member calls (or clicks) to make a reservation.

Likewise, the show does not end when the curtain closes. Disney knew, and now we know, that our show has many parts, and while the portion on the stage is important, everything that happens before it and after it are equally important. If we fail in one area, we risk damaging the product as a whole.

For example, when I visit a business prospect or potential donor to a charitable cause, I assume the person I am going to see is watching me from the window. When I arrive in the driveway or parking lot, I am ready to go. I am not checking messages as I get out of the car. My pace is quick (I can't wait to see the contact) and I am smiling. When I leave, I leave slowly. I hate to go. Whether the customer or donor is watching or not, as Walt Disney would say, he would "somehow know" that he was my sole focus, and that there was nothing more important in my day.

We should be mindful of our "show" because we don't always control when it begins. Human Relations offices are full of stories where candidates unknowingly cut-off the person in the parking lot who will be conducting the interview. Likewise, countless candidates have spoken poorly about the client or company they are visiting while in the hallway or elevator. Since we never know who is in the room or riding the elevator with us, we should always assume everyone is a V.I.P. and has the ability to hire us, fire us, or do business with us. Whenever we are on the way to an appointment or leaving an appointment, we are always on stage.

Once we get to the formal appointed meeting, we should make the person we are with feel he is the most important person in the world. Even if our day may be full of appointments, we want the person we are with to have our undivided attention. While he is certainly smart enough to know we will have other things to do that day, we want him to have the impression that while we may be doing other things before or after, nothing compares to the important time we are spending together.

Have you ever talked with someone on the phone and just knew they were smiling? You cannot see their face, but you just know. It is that feeling, that sense of knowing that everything is working together for the good of the whole, that Disney wants to convey.

Consider the "shows" we have all been part of, perhaps without realizing it. If you have ever seen a receptionist while waiting for a job interview, she is just as important as the person we are trying to see. More often than not, the supervisor who interviews us will talk with the receptionist after we leave and ask how we treated her.

The interview never begins when we sit down with the executive. It begins with how we treat the gatekeeper. Maybe the waiting room should be a safe area, since it is not really a part of the interview, but in reality the interview begins long before we hear the question, "Tell me a little about yourself." Everything matters. And how we treat the gatekeeper when making the appointment in the days and weeks before is just as important.

The same is true when others visit us. Interestingly, one of the people who is most important in many organizations is the one to whom we pay the least attention. The receptionist is the first impression for almost anyone that visits us. She sees every employee, guest, and delivery person. A good receptionist can make guests feel welcome and special. A good receptionist can get deliveries more quickly, and make employees feel better about their jobs. A poor receptionist can spread discontent like a rampant virus.

Every first impression we make should be a good one. To get that, we need to have good people in that position. When I go to local conferences I always try to bring my receptionist some of the cookies or treats we are given at lunch. For far-away conferences, I visit booths giving away freebies (or maybe I purchase a small souvenir) and bring something back for the receptionist and for other people who work for me and with me. It costs me nothing, or very little, but it shows I cared enough to find an item and bring it back.

That simple act shows the receptionist how important her work is, and how much a difference it makes. It would be okay to bring nothing back. However, when we do return with a small gift, we show we care.

Know Your Audience

Whether he was drawing a character with pen and ink, or designing an entire theme park, Walt Disney always had his customer in mind. No matter what he was working on, Walt focused his attention on how the ultimate consumer would view and receive his creation. He knew he had to appeal to the people who would buy a movie ticket, visit the theme park, or purchase a souvenir.

> **"You know what people want and you build it for them."**
> **— Walt Disney**

One of the great ironies of Walt's approach to customer service is that it is done so well, it is sometimes difficult to describe. An example of how this works is with computer-generated images in movies today. Hundreds or thousands of people toil endlessly on large movies to make sure the computer-generated images look perfect.

When they do their jobs well, we never notice. Filmmakers want you to forget you are watching a movie. They want you immersed in the story. If you stop to think about how realistic the spaceship looks, then the special effects have not done their job. Excellent movies are defined by their ability to make you forget you're watching a movie.

It is often the absence of distractions, not the presence of attractions, that defines greatness. Many of the best features in Disney's works are so seamlessly incorporated, it is likely most guests will never notice them. However, that does not mean they are not appreciated. Even though we may never think about how a particular scene in a movie or an attraction in a theme park is pleasing to us, we just somehow know it feels right and is good.

As we set out to please our audiences, we should remember that the better we do our jobs, the more likely it is they will not even notice we are doing our jobs. Just like special effects in movies, the things that are most important to our finished product are possibly never noticed. However, when they are missing or done poorly, those we serve will know. Some of our greatest investments in talent, production, and people will never be appreciated for their own sake. That's alright—because the product they produce will be. Greatly.

Window on Disney's World

One of the secrets to Walt Disney's success was his devotion to seeing things like his customers saw them. The mistake most businesses make is that they design a product or service, then attempt to sell it to the public. They create first, then figure out through focus groups and sales projections the best way to sell. Walt Disney approached things from the other direction.

Walt started with the consumer and observed what they wanted or needed. Today, the company still follows Walt's lead. It identifies a need and provides a solution to that need. It starts with the end in mind. When we think of our donors or customers first, we accomplish more.

An excellent example of anticipating and filling a need is the windows on Disneyland's Main Street, U.S.A.

Sometimes small changes we make to the way we do things can have a profound effect on ultimate results.

Walt designed those windows to be lower to the ground so small children could see inside the buildings.

Parents and their children will likely never notice or care about the height of the windows, even when they are designed to please them. Because Walt Disney alleviated a problem before it became one, he made his guests' shared experience that much better.

Parents would not have to pick up their children for them to look inside, and children would have an easier time seeing the temptations behind the windows so they could get their parents to take them inside and buy them. Not coincidentally, Disney also has a greater opportunity, and one less obstacle, to help families spend their money.

You could survey parents and children all day long, and none would ever tell you they appreciated the height of the windows. That does not mean it is unimportant. Some of our best ideas receive no direct feedback from our customers, donors, or consumers. Often, many of the finest things we do aren't "noticed" or commented on at all, but that does not mean they are not significant contributors to the bottom line. Be careful when assessing our actions. Lesser corporations and organizations are quick to dump ideas that cannot be directly proven or tested. Stick with what is right and go ahead, to paraphrase Davy Crockett.

Music to Your Customer's Ears

I was in a restaurant recently that had a really good sound system. The chain establishment was playing 1980s music over the sound system. It was pleasant and actually reminded me of my childhood and teen years. Apparently, the music I grew up with is now "retro," and I guess, *cool*. Duran Duran, Flock of Seagulls, and Men at Work are now considered oldies. When did that happen? But, it made me feel comfortable and happy as we walked to our table to sit down.

Another striking example of design from a child's point of view is the "Rags to Riches" statue of Cinderella near Cinderella Castle in Walt Disney World's Fantasyland. Behind the statue is an abstract painting with various images in it. If you look directly at Cinderella's face on the statue, one of the images on the painting behind her, a crown, is positioned perfectly to appear on her royal head— if you look from a child's perspective.

It quickly became apparent the comforting music playing throughout the restaurant was coming from a radio station. As such, it included commercials after every couple of songs. The first advertisement I heard was for a competing restaurant. The deep voice on the speaker was enticing me to try the "meats" at the other establishment.

Certainly the owner or manager of the restaurant where I was eating thought it would be nice to give guests familiar music. There might have even been some thought, or even research, into what type of music to play. Yet there I was, sitting in restaurant A, hearing a crystal-clear message for restaurant B.

At another local restaurant, the hostess at the door was wearing a t-shirt with the logo and slogan of a competing restaurant. Apparently, the dress code not only allowed t-shirts, but also did not seem to prohibit advertisements reminding you of another choice nearby. Unsurprisingly, the loyalty or disloyalty at the front desk was equaled when our food was served. The salad's lettuce was brown, the entrée was cold, and several ordered items were missing. At least the server had the sense to apologize for all the errors at the table.

The common theme with both the choice of radio station and the front-line attire is a lack of attention to the audience. In both cases, management, either by oversight or omission, decided that just providing music would be enough, and that just having employees who could walk you to your table would be sufficient. However, do we really want to remind our customers they could be somewhere else?

Guests Notice Everything

Businesses who make such oversights may survive, but they never thrive. The mistake these restaurants make, and the one we need to avoid, is that guests hear and see things we may not deem a priority. To combat this, we should always look at everything we do from our customer's perspective, not ours.

Walt Disney encouraged, if not demanded, his designers and Imagineers eat in Disneyland. He realized they would do their jobs better if they could see the people they were trying to please. He said, "Stand in line with the people...don't go off the lot to eat... you eat at the park and listen to people."

It serves us well to enter our workplace and read our materials from our customers' points of view. Talk with them. Listen. Watch. By entering through the front door, both literally and in our minds, and not through the employee entrance, we will gain invaluable insights into what is important and what needs to be changed or improved.

Above all, don't give our competition free advertising. Both organizations allowed their competitors into the heart of their business space. Not only had the competition directly infiltrated the walls of these establishments, but without even trying, they managed to advertise a competing product right under the nose of their rivals.

Douse Distractions

While it might be easy to excuse the radio station or the t-shirt as minor infractions, in Disney's world they would never happen. Disney immerses us in the Disney experience and never lets go. As we strive to make our corporation or organization better and more like Disney, we should search out anything that would distract our customer, donor, or audience.

While Disney never criticizes other entertainment companies, it also eliminates any reminders to customers they could find a product similar to Disney's anywhere else. For that reason, among others, Walt built a huge earthen berm and planted tall trees around the perimeter of Disneyland. Guests inside the park would not be distracted by the outside world.

When Walt planned Disney World, he bought

Leave no room for outside influences.

enough land so no one could build anything close enough to provide any distraction at all. At more than 47,000 acres, roughly twice the size of Manhattan, no other builder or developer can create any diversion that can be seen from Walt Disney World's theme parks.

In Orlando, critics say Disney's obsession with cleansing the parks of references to its competitors goes too far. When Walt Disney World opened, it had only two hotels on property. Today, guests can choose from more than 25,000 hotel rooms and campsites divided between 22 different hotels or resorts on property. Disney tempts guests to experience "the heart of the magic" by staying in a Disney resort on their trip to Orlando. Guests who stay on Disney property have a "more Disney" experience, and have fewer temptations to spend money on rooms, attractions, food, and souvenirs elsewhere.

There is nothing wrong with this, and other Orlando area theme parks are working hard to achieve the same kind of all-inclusive packaging. It makes good business sense. The common goal for the resorts is to never even let a guest think about leaving their properties. Disney has taken this one step further with pick-up and drop-off at the airport.

You can step off the plane and your bags are "magically" transferred directly from your airplane to your hotel room. Leaving is just as effortless with almost automatic transfers from your Disney resort to your plane. You can fly to Orlando and never step on land anywhere but the airport pick-up and Disney property—with no stops or diversions between.

We should do the same. When we work with customers or donors, we should give them a full experience. We don't need to criticize others, or even think of others. Just give our customer or donor a complete experience, and leave no room for them to think of anyone else that does what we do. Make our experience so full, so complete, that those we are with are so immersed in our story, they don't even need to think of anything or anyone else.

You Have No Competition

If you ask Disney who its competitors are, you may be surprised by the answer. Disney has no competition. At least, that's what Disney executives will tell you. There are simply no other organizations, companies, or people who do what they do. Sure, Disney is not naïve. There are movie companies making animated films and another movie studio spent more than a billion dollars to build a huge theme park less than ten miles from Walt Disney World.

However, Disney behaves as if it has no competitors because it does what it does so well. Walt Disney World's cast member handbook explains this in simple terms: "We don't have rides—they're for amusement parks." Disney breaks classifications and redefines categories.

Disney makes movies. Others make movies. Disney creates theme parks. So do others. Disney creates children's clothing and toys, and the list goes on and on. There is no area where Disney does not compete for dollars, yet Disney believes that while people are always free to spend money elsewhere, it has no direct competitors. No others do what Disney does, no matter what others say.

Disney believes so strongly in its products, and gives so much attention to the integrity and uniqueness of what it does, that no one has been able to match it. Others create roller coasters. Disney creates a rapid, turbulent attraction, Space Mountain, that simulates a trip through space. It succeeds. While others may do what we do, we must do it like no others. Do it like Disney.

Discover Your Excellence

We can all be like Disney. Even if we offer a product or service similar to those offered by others, we should remember our product and our mission are unique. Nothing we do should be interchangeable with what anyone else does. For example, if our mission is to feed the homeless, we shouldn't try to feed more people (although that is laudable), we should try to feed those we serve better. We feed them in a way that others wish to copy. It's all food. It's all delivery to people who need it. It's how we do it that counts. Even if our goal is to be the biggest, we shouldn't aim to do more. We aim to do better, and we grow bigger as a result.

Continuing to assume we are a food bank, our approach is not about taking a commodity, such as soup, and delivering it to those who are hungry. We must give the hungry our soup like no one else. For example, a charity in Huntsville, Alabama, sets up a table each day with a big soup kettle astride a linen table cloth on the enclosed porch of a local gourmet restaurant and places comfortable seats and a sign next to it that says: "Welcome. Soup."

The homeless who camp in the nearby woods can walk to the air-conditioned porch and eat for free with dignity. The same soup costs a lot more in an adjacent dining room for paying customers. The restaurant's homeless customers don't get soup in Styrofoam bowls. They receive warm, nutritious, homemade goodness that is served in china bowls with silverware and napkins, just like the paying clientele. Sure, others feed people—and do it well—but no one does it like this one. It serves dignity with every spoonful. The minimal extra cost is worth the self-esteem its clients feel.

To be like Disney, we must be exclusive content providers. Whatever we do, we should do it like no one else. We add magic to everything we do. To find our magic, concentrate less on what we do and more on how we do it. We approach our mission with flair and with an attitude that no one does what we do. Others may say they do, and we may even partner with organizations with similar missions, but we strive to find ways to fulfill our mission better and greater. We should never compete with anyone but ourselves.

What is the one thing you do better than anyone else? Focus on it. There is something your organization does better than all others. No matter what you have or what you lack, there are things you do better than everyone. That is your niche. That is your sweet spot. People will flock to you when you market that one thing.

Disney lives by this. Disney excels by this.

Mastering Magic

Walt Disney knew the power of magic. He was fascinated by the magician's ability to perform a seemingly impossible feat using practical techniques. He also had a deep appreciation for the audience. Above all, Disney recognized the two perspectives important in every magic trick; that of the magician and that of the audience.

While the audience sees a woman floating in mid-air, the magician sees a hidden lift and metal supports that make the trick work. Both perspectives are different, yet come together to give the audience a magical experience and the magician a paycheck.

Even standard magic tricks such as levitating the assistant or cutting the assistant in half never fail to win applause. That's because from the audience's point of view, the assistant seems to be floating on air, or to be cut in two at the waist. It never gets old.

We all know we are being tricked, but the magic is not in the seemingly impossible feat. The magic is in the entertainer's ability to make us forget we are watching an act. We *know* the assistant is still in one piece. We *know* the assistant is somehow suspended from the ceiling or lifted with some device. There is no cutting. There is no floating. The magic occurs when the magician has practiced and invested enough in the trick to make us suspend our well-placed disbelief. So it is with Disney.

We know there is no mouse five feet tall. We know a castle makes no sense on Main Street or any street in the U.S.A. However, the illusion is so complete, so magnificent, we are willing to allow our disbelief to take a rest for a while. Kings, queens, and heads of states have all posed for photos with Mickey Mouse. They were not posing with someone in a costume. It was (and is) Mickey Mouse. While our business may not have castles or costumed characters, we can none-theless benefit from these two perspectives by simply remembering we see the world from one point of view, and those we serve see it from another.

Make Magic

Always remember to make magic. Our business or organization's mission can be far from whimsy or amusement, and yet, it still needs magic. You can have a deadly serious business enterprise, but still benefit from magic's power.

I once asked a psychologist friend why his offices were all painted in dark, depressing colors. I had recently read studies on color selections and their effect on human behavior and emotion. The colors we choose in adver-tisements and the colors we use to paint walls have significant influence on our emotions and impulses. The psychologist friend said he had never thought about it. The walls were always just painted that way.

Even in his office, where people are suffering from depression, anxiety, or a host of other maladies, no one had thought about the effect colors had on their patients. And consider this: it was their profession that studied and affirmed that color choices matter.

Magic is not all fireworks and fantasy. Sometimes it is as simple as looking at our office from the perspec-tive of our patients. If we do, we will choose colors, furniture, and magazines that contribute to recovery and patient satisfaction rather than interfere with those successes.

Most of us are familiar with commercial aviation. You choose an airline and go to the airport and catch a flight. Usually, on the other side of the runway are facilities known as general aviation. General aviation is where smaller, private planes taxi and park. In all but the smallest airports, there are usually two or more competing companies that provide cleaning, fuel, and parking or hangar space for private aircraft. When a corporate pilot lands, for example, he or she can choose among several locations to leave the plane and have it serviced while on the ground. It is much like we would choose a parking garage or service station in a busy downtown area.

At general aviation offices, pilots can rent a car, hire cleaning services, or take a shower while waiting for their passengers to return from business meetings— and then fly everyone home.

One service and commodity almost all pilots need for their planes is fuel. Some of the general aviation companies noticed they were losing business to one competitor in particular. They discovered fuel sales were slumping even though their fuel was less expensive than the competition and delivered more quickly and cleanly to thirsty aircraft. These companies decided to study pilots to find out why they would go with another operator, even if it was more expensive.

At first it was a mystery. Why did pilots go past some operators and flock to others? Fuel is generally the same price and same quality at each of them. The first thing they discovered, but never previously considered, is that while a pilot may fly an executive for a certain company, that company rarely has a say in which ground operation the pilot should use. That decision is almost always left to the pilot.

What the companies found when they looked is that pilots were opting for the ground operations that offered the best pilot lounges and pilot facilities. The operators who were in the business of pleasing pilots were excelling. Those that concentrated on fuel were failing. Only a few operators were paying attention to their operations from the point of view of their customers, the pilots. When they did, they purchased more comfortable furniture, new carpet, and better televisions, and did more to attract pilots to choose their company. And pilots did.

What colors surround our spaces? What do we offer those we serve? What do people see and smell as they enter our offices? Most importantly, what feeling do they have when they enter our world, and what feeling do they have when they leave it? Remember, too, that "our world" could be a physical space, such as an office, theater, or hospital, but it could just as well be our postcard, our magazine, or the look of our suits and briefcases. In our world, as in Walt Disney's, everything matters, everything speaks. People make decisions for reasons personal to them, and some things we think don't matter much, matter a lot.

CHAPTER TWO

Widen Your World

Building Disneyland

Walter Elias Disney had nothing left to give. The year was 1953. Everything he had was about to ride on the success of his planned theme park, Disneyland, that would open in two years. To get the project started, Walt sold his vacation home in Palm Springs and borrowed $100,000 against his life insurance policies. He and his brother Roy leveraged every asset to pursue Walt's dream. Walt even borrowed money from several dozen studio employees.

For more than 20 years Walt had an idea for an "amusement enterprise" where parents could take their children. Unlike amusement parks at the time, where parents would sit on benches and passively watch as their children had

"Widen your World" comes from a lyric in the former Walt Disney World attraction, If You Had Wings. Disney replaced it with Buzz Lightyear's Space Ranger Spin, which uses much of the same track and show rooms of the former attraction.

fun, Walt wanted a place where parents and children could have fun *together*.

At the same time, children from all over the country had written to Walt wanting to know where Mickey Mouse lived. Walt was determined to build that magical land so he could take children and their parents to it.

His dream was to build them a Mickey Mouse Land. In 1953, the fate of the Disney studio (not to mention the Disney brothers' investment) hinged on the creation and success of Disney's Mickey Mouse Land. Having the idea for it, however, was in many ways easier than bringing it to life.

While most people associate the Disney brand with success, there was a time when Walt Disney was not a massive conglomerate. Disney was a man. And while he was arguably one of the greatest artists, business people, and leaders of the 20th century, his dreams were still just dreams, and like any of us and our dreams, it was possible that Mickey Mouse Land (later known as Disneyland) might forever be just a dream. Worse yet, the dream could sink the studio he and his brother worked so hard to build.

> "The idea for Disneyland came about when my daughters were very young, and Saturday was always daddy's day with the two daughters. I'd take them on the merry-go-round, sit on a bench... eating peanuts.... I felt there should be something built where the parents and children have fun together."
>
> — Walt Disney

Walt came up with the idea for Disneyland as he spent time with his daughters. Walt would often take them to Griffith Park in Los Angeles, where he would watch as they circled on the merry-go-round. He dreamed of a place where they could enjoy time together as a family. Rides and attractions would be designed for everyone and not just one generation or the other. His dream was Disneyland.

Today it's hard to imagine Disneyland was not a guaranteed triumph. It is almost impossible to even consider a time when it represented a real risk, let alone the possibility it would not be built. However, on the eve of its construction, the success of the planned theme park was still uncertain to everyone but the man who envisioned it.

A New Kind of Amusement Enterprise

In 1953, Walt's vision was coming into focus and his Magic Kingdom was about to become real. Despite the proven track record with previous Disney projects, his friends and rivals all had a name for Walt's land: Disney's Folly. However, with the same meticulous attention to detail displayed in Disney parks today, Walt Disney researched, studied, and asked questions to as many people as he could, to ensure the success of the new project. While his dream was conceived in ideals, it would be born from hard facts.

In late fall 1953, Walt Disney sent four of his best men to a convention of the National Association of Amusement Parks, Pools and Beaches. Dick Irvine, Nat Winecoff, Bill Cottrell, and Harrison "Buzz" Price met with four of the country's leading amusement park owners in a suite of hotel rooms at Chicago's Sherman Hotel on December 4. The Disney team assembled an impressive group of entertainment leaders:

- William Schmitt (Riverview Park in Chicago)
- Harry Batt (Pontchartrain Park in New Orleans)
- Ed Schott (Coney Island in Cincinnati)
- George Whitney (Playland at the Beach in San Francisco)

Gathering in the luxury rooms, the Disney representatives plied the other park owners with Chivas Regal and caviar. Filling them with fine drink and food, Disney's men wanted to extract as much information as they could about how to build an amusement park (until Disneyland, there was no concept of a "theme park" as there is today). The Disney experts, who knew a lot about movie-making, knew nothing about building a theme park. They wanted to see what the experts thought of Walt's idea.

Disneyland Would Be a Disaster

While Walt characteristically never wavered in his belief in the mission, the reports he received from Chicago that late fall had to give him second thoughts. His artists and managers were there to meet with successful amusement park owners, and what they heard was anything but encouraging.

For two hours the Disney team gave the amusement park owners a dog-and-pony show of the wonderful ideas they had for Disney's park. They showed the amusement professionals a prototype drawing of

Disneyland drawn by Disney artist Herb Ryman. It was a large-scale, photo-realistic aerial view that showed the park in its entirety. Ryman had drawn it to show potential investors what the park would look like.

Then the owners responded to Disney's team. They were loud. They were unanimous: "It would not work." The experts told Walt's hand-picked men that the planned park would be a catastrophe. It would bankrupt the whole Disney company along with the two men, Walt and his brother, Roy, who built it.

Disneyland Distress

As the amusement park owners explained their reaction, they told the Disney officials the park could never make money without traditional rides such as a roller coaster, tunnel of love, Ferris wheel, and hot dog cart. It also lacked the sure-fire moneymakers such as baseball throws or other carny games.

They said Disneyland would lose money with custom rides. They would be too expensive to build and maintain. Disney would need to have off-the-shelf rides like everyone else. Attractions like the pirate ship, castle, fire station, and town hall would be a waste of valuable real estate, as they produced no revenue. Lush landscaping was unnecessary and too expensive.

The owners also told Walt he was making a big mistake by having only one entrance. All their parks had multiple entrances.

Disney's park would also never make money by trying to stay open year-round. It should operate only for the summer season, like everyone else. They described Walt's ideas of cleanliness and attention to detail as "economic suicide."

Concluding their destruction of Walt's plan and his dream, they instructed the Disney representatives, as Buzz Price recounts in his book *Walt's Revolution! by the Numbers*: "Tell your boss to save his money. Tell him to stick to what he knows and leave the amusement business to people who know it."

Despite the clear advice from the amusement park owners, Disney went ahead with his plan for what would become Disneyland. The finished park, which opened two years later, would be built in much the same way as what the Disney leaders pitched to the park owners in Chicago. The large-scale drawing by Herb Ryman would bear an uncanny resemblance to the completed Disneyland. The finished park was almost identical to the drawing. Even more incredible

Sometimes experts are wrong. In the movie *The Poseidon Adventure*, there were two groups of potential survivors: one led by the ship's medic who was a crew member, the other led by a passenger, Reverend Scott (played by Gene Hackman). The larger group followed the medic because he should have known what to do. They died. The Hackman group survived because Hackman's character was creative and was willing to listen to a child who was fascinated with the structure and engineering of the ship. Sometimes the correct answer is not with the person who should know. Sometimes help comes from someone who knows the answer because they have passionately searched for it.

is that Ryman drew the entire layout in one weekend while he and Walt were locked in a room together until the drawing was done.

Despite the contrary expert advice from the amusement park owners in that Chicago hotel room, Disney would go on to employ two of the men as consultants. Walt Disney hired George Whitney and Ed Schott as advisors during the construction of Disneyland. In less than two years from the Chicago gathering, Disneyland would open to record-breaking crowds and worldwide acclaim.

Land the Dream

Disneyland now hosts millions of visitors each year. The men who knew the business better than Walt did not fare as well. Riverview Park in Chicago went out of business in 1967. San Francisco's Playland closed in 1972, and Pontchartrain Park in 1983. Only Ed Schott's Coney Island in Cincinnati remains open and vital.

The experts who told Walt Disney's leaders to abandon the theme park idea are not unlike the experts you might encounter on any given day. Everyone has an opinion and while they are quick to form them, they are even faster forcing them on you. Although the words, "That's the way we've always done it," are dangerous, the more dangerous words are, "That's the way everyone else is doing it." Avoid the temptation to follow others, or choose the ones you follow carefully.

The four experts in the room insisted Walt do it their way. Theirs was the only way, and they listed dozens of reasons why it was. The Disney creative team was new to the idea and was not reluctant to confess their inexperience.

While Walt Disney showed them how his park would be different, he also revealed how everyone he would ostensibly be competing against did things the same way. They were unanimous in everything they said and did to bash Walt's dream.

The voices of the men who gave that advice to Walt in 1953 still echo today. Whether it is your board, your volunteers, your employees, or even your donors or customers, there is no shortage of people to pour cool water on the flames of creativity. There is a lot we can learn from Walt's approach to Disneyland, and in his response to the experts.

To Create a New Dish, Don't Use the Old Recipe

Albert Einstein is often quoted as saying: "To keep doing the same thing and expect a different result is insanity." Walt Disney knew from the start he wanted a park different from all others. He also knew that to achieve a park different from others, he would have to start differently. He would have to design differently. He would have to do everything differently.

If we want our organization or business to be better than others, we can't do everything they are doing and expect different results. We can never be better than someone else by copying them. If we only do what others are doing, or worse, what they did, then at best we can equal them. To be better we must be like Disney. Watch the competition, watch those who have gone before us, but to be better we need to try harder, and do it a little differently.

When Walt Disney's team consulted the experts,

they could have done what most people do. They could take a few of the successes from the history of the other amusement parks and combine them into something new. Disney took a different approach. Rather than copy them, he sent his team to interview them, much like a reporter would.

Walt wanted to glean knowledge and experience and not simply copy what they had done. He was looking for their weaknesses more than their strengths so he could be sure Disneyland did not repeat their mistakes. He wanted to know what they knew but not necessarily follow their lead.

When we set out to build a new product or to look for ways of doing anything better, we should be bold enough to contact those who have gone before us. Often they are competitors. As Walt and his team proved, there is great value in harvesting the knowledge of those who have done something similar to what we plan to do.

But as we learn from them, it is only a starting point, not a recipe to follow. The accomplishments of our competitors are their past achievements. They should never be our future goals. If we only want to be like them, we should quit our company and join theirs. If we want to be better than them (or at least different), we should learn from

If you are in a meeting and someone asks what another similar organization is doing so you can do the same thing, that is a sign you are settling for mediocrity or at best a poor facsimile of what someone else has already done.

their mistakes and their victories, and improve on both. While it sounds like common sense, it is uncommon to see this observed in business today.

And while Disney is arguably at the pinnacle of customer service and excels in creativity, other corporations and organizations share the same spirit. Southwest Airlines, consistently ranked as one of the most popular domestic airlines, understands how to approach customers. In an article on workforce.com by Brenda Paik Sunoo, entitled "How Fun Flies at Southwest Airlines," the company shows the priority it places on hiring people with personality and then training them in the skills they need to perform their job well.

Southwest's former president and CEO, Herb Kelleher, said, "What we are looking for, first and foremost, is a sense of humor. We look for attitudes. We'll train you on whatever you need to do, but the one thing we can't do is change inherent attitudes in people." Southwest hires the smile and trains the skill.

If you are in the service industry or work for a non-profit organization in any role, you are in one of the few positions and professions where *who you are matters as much or more than what you know*. Employers looking to hire someone to stitch a shirt or change the oil in a car usually don't look for personality, they want skill. However, who you are is important. No amount of skill can replace a great attitude in our business.

One of the best things we can do is invest in each other. As Ken Blanchard wrote in his book *Legendary Service*, "Great companies realize their most important customers are their own people—employees and managers. If leaders take care of their people and encourage them to bring their brains to work, the people will go out of their way to take care of customers." Increasingly, companies are discovering when they focus on their employees that guest, customer, or donor satisfaction increases almost automatically.

Good People Solve Bad Problems

July 17, 1955, was opening day at Disneyland; it came to be known as "Black Sunday." Even before dawn, as guests were lining up in the parking lot and backing up streets for miles in Orange County, workers were still pouring hot asphalt on Main Street and aligning a 900-pound elephant in the Jungle Cruise. Construction continued even as guests entered the park.

The invited guests overwhelmed the park's infrastructure, and the Disney team soon discovered there were many uninvited guests as well. Disney had printed 11,000 park passes for employees, family, and friends. They wanted to make sure there were plenty of people so the live television broadcast would depict a park full of happy, smiling faces. The invitations were sent thinking that few would come. They were wrong.

People started lining up along the roads and freeways in the middle of the night. Streets were clogged by daybreak. The passes that Disney printed were easily forged, so many more people came than they expected. Instead of the 11,000 anticipated guests, more than 28,000 showed up.

According to David Koenig in *Mouse Tales*, Disney employees found one man who had set up a ladder over the berm near the back of the property and was charging people $5 to use it to sneak into the park. Many of the attractions broke down or had no electricity. There were too few trash cans, not enough food, and following a plumber's strike, Disney had a choice late in the construction: install toilets or install water fountains. He chose to install toilets, which led to (unfounded) speculation that it was done on purpose so people would buy more Pepsi which the park sold. Stories abound about opening day troubles, including women's shoes sinking into the still-wet asphalt and ample missed cues during the live television broadcast.

Despite these problems, Disney stuck with his dream. More food was ordered, more trash cans were placed in the park, and many of the other problems were quickly solved, or at least were on their way to being solved. Even with the opening day calamities, and surely the negative words of the other experts echoing in Disney offices, Walt Disney, along with the corporation and park he built, persevered. Walt believed enough in his project to stick with it. The public rewarded him for his effort. Disneyland passed the one million visitor mark within seven weeks of opening.

No Request Is Too Extreme

Of all Walt Disney's projects, Disneyland was probably his most personal. It was in his blood. It had been waiting to be birthed for decades. He thought about it daily. Only his dream of EPCOT, perhaps, was dearer to him than Disneyland. Yet, despite Walt's emotional and financial investment in the project, he was not there in that Chicago hotel room to meet the experts. Instead, he sent his trusted team.

Walt was shrewd enough to know his dream was bigger than him and he would need the influence, perspective, and expertise of others. He valued his team's energy and attitude. He also had the sense to ask others in the field, the would-be experts. While he ultimately chose not to follow their advice, he listened. And despite largely ignoring their counsel and building Disneyland as he had always intended, he later hired two of the amusement park owners as consultants.

When we set out to sell a product or service or raise money for our organizations, whether we are the CEO or a new hire in a part-time job, we should carefully consider the perils of "going alone." Walt demonstrated the virtues of seeking and considering the advice of others. Walt showed the value in assembling a great team of people with various levels of talent, skills, and abilities. He also trusted them to engage other experts. And perhaps most notably, he asked the competition what he should do. Even rivals can offer advice and a point of view that aids us.

Whittle While You Work

Walt was also good at turning problems into publicity opportunities. He seemed to thrive on adversity. One such example was the story of how Disneyland lost "all" its trees at a critical time before opening day.

During the construction of Disneyland, landscaping supervisors tagged trees on the Disneyland property with ribbons. One color ribbon indicated a tree was to be untouched, another meant destroy, and another meant relocate. All work was to be done by bulldozer. Apparently, the bulldozer operator was color blind and destroyed all the trees at Disneyland. Where he saw a ribbon, he simply took down the tree. It was a disaster. At least that's the way the Disney public relations department portrayed it.

While it's true there was a color-blind bulldozer operator and many trees were destroyed that should have been saved or relocated, the reality was far less dramatic than Disney's publicity department portrayed. The damage was limited to a small area in Adventureland and was relatively harmless. Although the damage was minimal, the story was milked for maximum impact.

When the Disney publicity team heard about the destruction of the trees, they played it up. They described the damage as extending to every tree on the property. It made an amusing story that captivated the press and heightened interest in Disneyland long before opening. Disney's ability to create tall tales from short stories was already well-honed long before Disneyland opened. They turned failure into an opportunity.

While it is easy to think that Disneyland was always a guaranteed success, it wasn't. As we plan and deal with projects, events, and marketing, we can follow Disney. Even with the greatest creative minds in the country, problems still happen. Problems will happen for us as well. Like Disney, it's how we handle them that matters. The next time someone bulldozes "all" your trees, remember it may be the end of one story, but it is also the beginning of another.

Guests Will Tell Us What They Want

Do we listen to our donors, customers, and guests like Disney listens to theirs? When Disneyland opened, guests paid $1 for general admission, then another ten to thirty-five cents for each attraction. The cost depended on the attraction. Within a few months, Disney introduced a ticketing system that would become part of the American lexicon. At first there were "A," "B," and "C" tickets. The best rides were "C" tickets. "A" rides were the ones your tried when the lines were too long at the "B" and "C" attractions. Later, the "D" ticket was introduced as the Magic Kingdom expanded. Finally, in 1959, Disney completed the ticket book with a term we still use today to describe something awesome or incredible: the "E" ticket.

The "E" ticket represented the best Disney had to offer. In 1959, it included attractions such as the Matterhorn Bobsleds, Submarine Voyage, and Jungle Cruise. Later "E"-ticket attractions were Big Thunder Mountain Railroad and the Haunted Mansion. However, by June 1982 the words that would last forever in American culture disappeared from Disney guests' hands. Like other theme parks that were starting to become popular around the country, Disney abandoned the ticket system.

Despite the success of the ticket books, Disney learned guests did not like carrying them around, and more importantly, they did not like being told they could only ride certain attractions a limited number of times (although you could always buy additional tickets). So, in response to guest questions and complaints, in June 1982 Disney sold its last book of tickets. Once guests were in the park, they could ride what they wanted as much as they wanted, as long as they were willing to stand in line. Although Disney pioneered the attraction ticket book, they were willing to give it up when guests told the company they wanted more freedom and flexibility.

The Disney company's ability to listen to its customers, or guests, is one of the things that sets the organization apart so distinctly from others. Rather than try to wow customers with additions or renovations that are the biggest, fastest, or most gigantic, Disney instead takes cues from its customers and fascinates them in an untold number of small, but personal ways.

Define Your Excellence

You might be surprised to learn that Disneyland and Walt Disney World don't set many records. You will not ride the fastest roller coaster in the world in a Disney park. You will not find the highest roller coaster in a Disney park, nor will you see the longest roller coaster in a Disney park. Even for all its many rides, shows, and attractions, Disneyland (or any Disney park) rarely sets records for anything in any category, except one.

The one record Disney holds is the only one that counts: attendance. As explained in the Disney Institute book *Be Our Guest*, by 1996 an estimated 1.2 billion people had visited a Disney park. In that year, Disney's largest property, Walt Disney World, boasted 27 hotels with more than 25,000 rooms, as well as 300 restaurants and eateries.

People don't come to Disney parks to ride the fastest, tallest, or scariest of anything. There are plenty of other places for those chills and thrills. Disney's lands provide an overall experience, and give guests something more: a story. Consider that when Disneyland opened in 1955 it had no thrill rides at all. It was only with the addition of the Matterhorn in 1959 that Disney added a roller coaster to its stable of attractions.

While the Matterhorn did not set speed or height records, it did set one important Disney-type record. It was the first roller coaster in the world to be made of steel tubing and it was the first to have "blocks" or sections so multiple trains could safely be on the track at the same time. Records for being the first at something can never be broken. Disney rarely sets out to be the most of something. "Most" things can always be overcome with more. Firsts, however, are firsts forever. It takes more effort, dedication, and courage to be the first at anything, but as Disney shows, the rewards are often worth it.

Set the Right Records

Think about the records you want to set. The theme of far too many board meetings and subsequent staff meetings is "how can we be the most" of something? There is always a struggle, if not a competition, to serve more people, build more buildings, or expand into new areas.

Sometime around 1990, and lasting for ten or so years, theme parks in the United States and around the world found themselves in what industry insiders called a "roller-coaster arms race." During that time, one theme park would build a roller coaster that included some exciting new feature. It might be the most loops, the highest drop, or the fastest speed.

Each summer season brought the unveiling of a new type of roller coaster. Some innovations and openings came so quickly that a theme park that began the summer with the fastest coaster would find itself in second place by Labor Day.

There were stand-up coasters, then really tall coasters called megacoasters or hypercoasters. Later, even taller coasters demanded a new name: gigacoaster. When enough gigacoasters started appearing everywhere a new category emerged: stratacoaster. No one could design, build, or test the maximum limits of thrills without being topped by another soon after.

One could say the roller-coaster arms race ended only when theme park operators discovered there were limits to what the human body could withstand. One theme park near London was forced to redesign a ride after a particularly revealing pre-opening test run. As told in a *Los Angeles Times* article, "Thrill Ride Designers Compete to Push the Limits," by Hugo Martín, several mannequins used to test the new attraction lost limbs as they rode the rails.

During the 1990s, as other theme parks raced to outdo each other, Disney watched. Even as then-Disney CEO Michael Eisner declared the 90s to be the Disney Decade, Disney's theme parks clearly did not participate in the coaster wars. During that so-called Disney Decade, the company built only three coasters in the United States: Gadget's Go Coaster in Disneyland (top speed 21.7 mph), Goofy's Barnstormer in the Magic Kingdom (top speed 25 mph), and the Rock 'n' Roller Coaster at Disney-MGM Studios in Orlando (top speed 57 mph). Disney's investment in thrills was negligible compared to its competition, if you considered the competition to be other theme and amusement parks.

Like any other arms race, there were winners and losers. Some theme parks could not keep up. Some went out of business. Some filed bankruptcy. The same is true for the companies that designed and built roller coasters. Disney remained strong, choosing to compete where others weren't: in story telling, cleanliness, and dedication to customer service.

Where do we compete? Just because others are doing the same thing does not mean we should. Disney survived and thrived because it had something no one else had. Disney had wonder. Disney had enchantment. Disney had magic.

While Disney cares as much about the bottom line as any corporation (profit or nonprofit), it is extraordinarily careful when setting benchmarks for itself. It rarely boasts the biggest, longest, or fastest of anything. When it does advertise in superlatives, it is almost always in terms of the giving the best guest experience possible. Racing to be the record holder in anything leads only to disappointment. Set a record and someone will immediately try to beat it.

CHAPTER THREE

First Impressions Last

Most Important Job in the Park

In about my sixth year as a seasonal employee at Busch Gardens in Tampa, I had the best job in the world. I had finally been granted the position I always wanted: steam train engineer. It was a much sought-after position. Many of the other engineers had been there for years. As an employee who only worked summers, weekends, and holidays (while I was in high school and college), it was difficult to get a job on the train. But that summer, I had my opportunity.

Being an engineer was a fun job, but it was also more complicated than it appeared, and had a significant element of potential danger. In addition to the obvious concerns about the train hitting a guest, zoo animal, or car at one of several employee road crossings, there was also the mechanics of running a huge steam engine. Operating a train that carries tons of weight and five hundred passengers was daunting but always exciting. I even got to blow the whistle!

The fireman on the left side of the cab controlled water to the boiler (the long, huge cylinder that makes up most of the locomotive) that would heat at high pressure. He would control the boil by timing the adding of water from the tender as well as the intensity of the huge flame that shot from a spout within inches of both our feet. The flame was visible, real, and always right there. Even in cold winters, the cab was consistently toasty.

The engineer sat on the right side of the cab and was responsible for moving and stopping the train as well as being the primary communicator with the stations, maintenance, and other trains. At Busch Gardens, the engineer and fireman would also alternate working both positions to give some variety to the day.

Being in the locomotive cab was so important it came with an automatic pay increase called "hazard pay." To run the engine, I had to study for and pass an intensive City of Tampa boiler license exam. However, the effort was worth it. In the decades since, I have yet to experience anything that produced the thrill of pulling back on the throttle and feeling all that machinery move at my command. It was amazing. It was fun.

Promotion Emotion

I had been on the engine for a little more than a month and was having the time of my life when a manager approached me. He asked if I would consider being a supervisor in the parking lot. He told me I would be perfect for the job and I could keep my hazard pay increase and consider it a raise for my work as a supervisor. While he painted the transfer in rosy terms, he was asking me to leave a job I loved.

The parking lot at Busch Gardens, like any theme park, is massive. It is a couple dozen acres of deep, dark, black asphalt. The tar-and-rock mixture is the perfect sponge to soak up every inch of Florida's summer sun. It absorbed so much heat that it had plenty to spare and would reflect back much of it all day long, releasing that stored-up heat well into the night. While the high temperature was a common companion, the long, scorching days were pierced by something Florida experiences almost daily in the summer: torrential thunderstorms.

The lightning was spectacular, but because we had to help guests come and go when they chose, we rarely closed the parking lot. As I heard the walkie-talkies tell of the other attractions closing because of bad weather, we kept right on moving cars into and out of the parking lot and shuttling guests to and from the front gate. It would take the threat of a tornado or very close lightning to make us stay off the lot. Other attractions seemed to close if lightning was reported in a nearby county, but we kept going for as long as we could.

The special part of Florida being the lightning capital of the world is that the storms are usually hard, but almost always brief; usually less than an hour. In addition to the heat generated before the storm, the parking lot would release steam for hours, or until the next storm came along to recharge the whole process. But the weather was not the only special consideration of the parking lot.

Parking lot employees are among the first to arrive in the early morning and the last to leave late at night. Supervisors have to report even earlier and leave later than the employees. Not only do parking lot employees work in the most demanding positions, they also have to do it for the longest hours.

So, I was confused and concerned when an area manager told me transferring to the parking lot would be a good move if I chose to stay at Busch Gardens. He said it was the *most important* position in the park. I did not believe him, but after accepting the position (I really was not given a choice, although it was presented as one), I quickly agreed. He said the parking lot was the most important position because you would set the first impression for each guest and be the last impression each would remember before heading home.

He was right.

It did not take long to see the smiles and excitement in the morning. I got to be the one that pulled back the curtain for every guest. Almost no one would enter the park without seeing me or one of my employees. Our smiles, our waves, and our courtesy set the tone for each and every visitor. A pleasant and prompt tram ride from the guest's car to the entrance set the expectation that every other ride that day would be the same. The opposite was also true.

Besides, working in the parking lot was more fun than I thought it would be. The cast members were exceptional and it was a joy to work with them. I became proficient at driving big trams, and I also got to interact with the outside world more regularly than did other cast members. I also became proficient at breaking into cars and jump-starting dead batteries (skills I might one day re-employ if the writing and speaking thing ever stops working for me).

Carefree guests would lock their keys in their cars. Several times throughout the day, as a supervisor, it was my job to help them get back in. I could pop certain car doors in seconds. Similarly, if you left your lights on and drained the battery, I could get you up and going in minutes. You could not be a bigger hero than by opening locked doors and reviving stalled cars, especially if you could accomplish it with a smile and without embarrassing the guest.

That summer in the Busch Gardens parking lot taught me lessons that last today. Whether we work in a department store, restaurant, or parking lot, we must always remember that our guest's first impressions last. The people we have on the front line, as well as the parking lots, front entrances, and waiting areas are all probably far more important than they otherwise would be. At the same time, having the friendliest, most responsive people answering phones, opening doors, and responding to emails is crucial.

In recent years I have discovered that a good smile shines through even in a customer email or online chat. The key is to remember that the cliché is true: we never really do get a second chance to make a first impression. Walt Disney knew the power of first impressions, which is why he spent so much time designing one land in his park, an area most of us never even consider a land at all: Main Street, U.S.A.

A Grand Entrance

As you enter the Magic Kingdom, whether in Anaheim or Orlando, Main Street, U.S.A. is your first impression. Ask any child which land is the most important in any Disney park, and Main Street would not be high on the list—if at all. Back when there were "E" tickets, there was not a single "E"-ticket attraction on Main Street. However, Walt Disney paid a lot of attention to Main Street, as do all managers and Imagineers today.

But even while children may not notice Main Street, and adults may not appreciate it, that single street sets the stage for your entire park experience. In many ways, it is the most important land in any Disney park. It has the distinction of being the first and last area guests see, other than the parking lot.

It sets the tone for the day. And at the end of a long day, it is the visual snapshot that will be among the last from what was hopefully a wonderful visit. Main Street was immensely important to Walt Disney. The lessons from this stretch of pavement are important for us, too.

Walt Disney and Imagineer Harper Goff designed Main Street as Walt Disney remembered the Main Street from his childhood in Marceline, Missouri, and his early life in Kansas City. Harper Goff grew up in Collins, Colorado. Main Street, U.S.A. is a reflection of both men's childhoods.

They did not design their Main Street as a *replica* of the Main Streets in Marceline, Collins, or Kansas City. Main Street, U.S.A. represents a visualization of Walt's memory. It is Main Street as he perceived it to be. It is more of an impressionistic painting than a photograph. It represents the common memory of the way many of us believe the world once was. Disney designed it to evoke nostalgic memories, not faithfully recreate turn-of-the-19th century America.

Walt realized that many of his guests had never been to Marceline or Kansas City. Since decades had passed, those cities no longer existed either, at least as they were when he was young. Yet the images are so compelling they are represented in all of Disney's magic kingdoms around the globe.

The Star of the Show

Walt Disney designed his theme park as a living motion picture. Accordingly, everything on Main Street, U.S.A. progresses like a movie. As you enter from the parking lot, all you can see is the train station, with maybe the spires of the castle peeking out behind. You hear noises and smell candy, but the train station prevents you from fully seeing what lies beyond. The show has not yet begun, but you do have a taste of what you are about to experience.

As you pass under the train station you are in a dark tunnel, much like the way a theater darkens as the show begins. Along the tunnel walls you see posters for many of the rides and shows in the park. These are literally the coming attractions.

As you emerge from the tunnel it is the same as as the opening dissolve in a movie. Darkness opens up to reveal a lively, moving setting. The experience continues with a popcorn stand always positioned just beyond the train station that is open any time the park is open. Just like the movies, there will always be popcorn there.

The difference with Disney is that you are not watching a movie. You are in it. And you are the star.

As you enter Main Street, you may notice the sidewalks are red. The hue represents a red carpet; *your* red carpet. You are the guest of honor when you enter this Magic Kingdom and the street reflects your importance.

When designing Main Street, Disney consulted Kodak. As Susan Veness explains in her book *The Hidden Magic of Walt Disney World*, Disney and Kodak worked together to come up with a shade of red that contrasted best with the green grass and other nearby colors. With this setting presented so perfectly for you, it's difficult to take a bad photo on Main Street, U.S.A. The castle at the end of Main Street is also aligned so the sunshine lights it perfectly for you.

As you walk down Main Street and toward the castle, you also move forward in time. The train station represents America of the late 19th century. As you walk you move from that century to the early 20th century. The gas lights along the street are subtly replaced by electric lights as you get closer to the castle. The transition is like a dissolve in a movie where one scene fades and another emerges.

The transition also helps sell the possibility of a huge castle and a "Tomorrowland" adjacent to an antiquated Main Street. Main Street features many other details and imagery that help set the stage for the day's visit.

While none of us have our own Main Street, U.S.A. as the first impression for our guests, customers, or donors, we *do* have first impressions. Whether they set us up for failure or success is up to us.

What Is Our Main Street?

While no one but Disney has Main Street, U.S.A., we all have front doors, websites, and phone numbers. The style, emotion, and ease-of-use of all these tell our customers, donors, volunteers, and guests more about us than just about anything we can do.

We should build everything from a donor's or customer's point of view. Just as Disney's theme parks would not exist without guests, our businesses and nonprofits would be out of business without customers and donors. Everything we do should be done from their perspective.

Start at the beginning: with our first impressions.

How can we determine if our organization has the right perspective? Look at it from the point of view of someone who is new to it. Approach it as a prospective customer or donor.

What do people hear when they call us? Let's say we need information from Fred about an upcoming event. So we call him, and instead of reaching him, we hear a voicemail with Fred's voice. First, we should realize that getting a voicemail already puts the caller at a disadvantage.

The caller wanted Fred, and instead got a message that Fred was "away from his office or on another line." The unspoken part of that message is that no matter what Fred is doing it is more important than talking to you. While it may be acceptable in business today to screen calls or ignore incoming calls, is "acceptable" the standard we want to meet?

Disney does not usually settle for acceptable. To achieve Disney results, we must work for something more. Acceptable is unacceptable. Good enough is never good enough. But, back to the call. After hearing all the reasons why Fred cannot talk with us, we leave a message. We wait in line. Fred will call us back (maybe) when he is no longer away from his desk or on another call.

At least once a month, I hear this recorded greeting: "I am away from my desk or on another call, but will return your call at *my earliest convenience...*" I

Good is never good enough.

cringe when I hear this. "*Your* convenience?" Who is more important: the caller or the person being called? It might be a simple misstep in hurriedly recording an outgoing message, but excellence is not achieved at Disney by doing anything at the convenience of the employees.

Disney's motto is: "We work while others play." In the same way, we must treat every call as incoming business. While it is "work" to answer the phone or return calls promptly, such attention to detail and seeing the world from the customer's point of view is essential to the Disney way.

Disney knew, and his company knows, it is we that serve the customer (or donor) and not the other way around. It is not our convenience that matters. It is that of the caller. The caller may want to make a donation or sign the deal. The caller may be calling to say "yes" to our requested appointment. The caller could be someone who needs us. We forget, because our corporate culture does not encourage us to remember, that our outgoing message should reflect the right attitude.

Often, outgoing messages are something recorded as an "oh yeah, that's one more thing we need to do" on the first day of employment. In some cases, the outgoing message is recorded on our behalf before we even start. Yet that message is in many cases our first impression, our billboard, our calling card. If they cannot reach us, then our placeholder, the outgoing message, should do a good job representing us.

While the outgoing message is crucial, the return call is no less important. Calls should be returned promptly. Even the difficult ones. Especially the difficult ones. That tells the caller they are important.

When we don't, the caller begins to associate us with not caring, being lazy, or even narcissistic. While it may be common in today's business world to screen calls and take our time returning them (if at all), we have to do things others don't.

And here's a bonus. Take the tough calls. No matter what business we are in, we all have calls no one wants to take. These are the calls where someone wants to complain or whine about some disappointing interaction with you or your company. I have seen these calls shoved to terminal hold, or transferred to a station where no one is. No one wants to take them. Except you, now.

If you want to be a hero in your organization, be the one who jumps up and volunteers to take the difficult calls. Whether you are the owner of the company or it's your first day on the job, others will like you and respect you more when you give them a place to send the stinky calls. However, these tough calls are rarely tough.

The problem is when most people take the complaint calls, they argue back. They respond to the fight with more fight. Both sides dig in, and the call sinks into a nasty debate that only gets worse each minute. Who would want to take that call?

When presented with an irate customer or contact, take the call, and just listen. Occasionally express mutual sadness with the caller's disappointment. Empathize. You do not need to lie or accept unnecessary blame, or agree to anything inappropriate or misleading. However, at a minimum it is alright to empathize with someone who has had a bad experience, even when they created that experience themselves.

As you listen to the caller, just agree that the person has a valid reaction to a perceived bad time. Don't make excuses. If the person is unstable or unreasonable, clearly you do not have to endure such a call. But in most cases the caller has a simple message: they loved us more than we loved them. They invested something in us (cash, time, or trust) and we did not value it enough. When someone calls to complain about such an issue, there is nothing we can say to alleviate the pain, other than empathizing.

Just the simple act of listening and agreeing that if you were in the other person's shoes you might have a similar reaction comforts the caller. They may not have a "valid" complaint, but you can never argue with their reaction to it. By listening to the caller you will be a hero to the customer and to your fellow employees.

The customers we should be truly concerned about are the ones who don't call. Rather, they tell their friends and neighbors how badly we performed and never give us an opportunity to respond. Those situations cause real harm and the only thing we can do to prevent them is to create an atmosphere where guests and customers know their complaints will be heard and addressed.

Disney puts its best and brightest cast members in Guest Relations for a reason. They have the ability to listen to a guest complain, and while doing so, craft a solution that pleases that guest while also protecting the company.

Learn from Experience: How Not to Treat Donors

A few years ago I was invited to speak in a city where I knew a number of people. This was a favorite part of the country for me so I was eager to accept and speak there to a group of non-profit organizations on how to improve donor relations. I loved this area so much, I brought my family with me and we even took a couple of days off after the speech to enjoy a mini-vacation.

The day after my speech, I took my family to a local attraction, which also happens to be a non-profit, donation-seeking organization. It was a cross between a zoo and a scientific research facility (that accepts and helps heal certain wild, marine animals). This is a popular attraction and I knew the head fundraiser there.

Knowing we would visit the next day, I went on the internet in our hotel room the night before and purchased for my wife, sons, and me an annual family membership; the highest level of affiliation one could have. Even though it was 900 miles from our home and we would likely not visit again for years, I thought it would be nice to support the facility and my friend who worked there.

The next morning, we showed up early. We were the first car in the parking lot. As we saw people starting to stir behind the turnstiles we went to the gate to be first in line. We were excited and my young sons could not wait to get in. Within a few moments a long line formed behind us.

As the park opened, I went to the member booth. I told the representative I had purchased an annual family membership. She asked me for a printout of my confirmation. This was before smartphones and tablets. The hotel where we stayed did not have a printer I could use, nor did I pack one in my suitcase. I told her I was without a printout, but told her I received a confirmation email and gave her other information that made it clear we were new members.

Golly, What a Day

She told me I could not get in without a printout. She was quite upset we did not have a printed confirmation and called another employee over. The second employee arrived and even though we were within feet of both ladies, she never made eye contact or acknowledged us in any way. With both their backs turned to us, the second lady shook her head as the two employees debated what to do next.

They called their supervisor.

The supervisor arrived and this was clearly an annoyance to her. The three talked, then the supervisor turned and chastised me in front of my children for not having a printout. She explained that the ticketing process is "handled by another company," and they don't get notice of new memberships for days. She said she would let us in "this time," but next time we "better have a printout, or she would not let us in."

The day was ruined for us. We had taken the step to elevate the experience to the best it could be. We were not only customers. We were donors. We were members. Anyone could pay a minimal fee and enjoy the park for the day. We took the extra step and paid far more than was necessary.

Even though that day was years ago, I remember it vividly. We did not renew, although we do still get mail asking us to give. While it would be easy to blame the front-line employees, their attitudes reveal something deeper and more troubling. The organization does not value donors or customers. Or at least, it does not value them as much as they should.

Since the organization would not exist if it weren't for the donors, it's important that the organization value its donors more highly. There are several ways of solving this problem. The leadership could:

- Tell front-line people, especially staff that deal directly with guests or donors, that there are better, more personal ways of dealing with new customers or donors. While one could argue we were treated the way we were because they did not believe us, that was never the issue. They had enough clues that they never doubted we were members. What they knew was that we did not have the proper form, and they were not trained how to respond when the proper form was not presented. They gave the form more importance than the humans in front of them.

- Work with membership vendors for better ways of communicating with the organization so that this would not happen again.

While these two options should be employed by the organization (and re-evaluated regularly), they are only temporary fixes. Staff will come and go and so will vendors. Any training or improvements made in the system tend to leave with them. However, an overall attitude of appreciating customers or donors sticks around.

Any Happy Little Thought

I envision the first day on the job for those folks we encountered that day. Someone, perhaps another employee at their level, told them the most important thing anyone in that position could do is keep the paperwork straight. It is not a stretch to imagine some former employee being disciplined for not turning in the right forms at the end of a shift. There must have been severe consequences. The charity emphasized then, and continues to place priority now, on paperwork.

However, there is a third option and one that Disney excels in implementing throughout its corporation. From the first moment an employee ("cast member" in the case of Disney) is hired, the employee is educated in the history, traditions, and priorities of the company.

When Disney trains employees, it begins and ends with the guest experience. Everything supports a positive guest experience or it is weeded out of the system. Likewise, people who do not support a positive guest experience are not hired, or are soon out of the company.

The front-line staff that day at the charity were probably told to be polite, look nice, and learn various

> If the answer to any guest question or complaint is, "Sorry, but that's our policy," then something is wrong. Simply telling a guest that they're in violation of a rule is inappropriate. Even if the guest is wrong it is better to explain the reasoning behind the policy rather than just stating a rule.

places they could point guests who needed help (lost and found, first aid, etc.). That was all they were told about the guest experience. What the charity never realized was that these employees had more to do with the guest experience, and even donor relations, than the management, the supervisors, or even the fundraisers on staff.

At Disney it's all part of the show and everyone's a performer. If you have front-line staff, let them know how important their roles are. Remind them they have more contact with donors and potential customers than anyone else in the organization. If you are front-line staff, know that your attention to the guest will be rewarded quickly. If it is not, you are probably not working for the right organization and need to find a better job.

We don't have to give front-line staff free range to accomplish guest satisfaction. But we do need to provide opportunities to them to give donors and potential donors a positive, if not delightful, experience. As part of the training, we should remind them everyone is a V.I.P. Forms, policies, and procedures are important, but the guest is more important. We must:

- Look at front-line staff (receptionists, custodians, volunteers)

According to the Disney employee guide *The Magic is You! A Guide to Your Role in the Show*, there are only three "Misters" in the Magic Kingdom: Mr. Lincoln, Mr. Toad, and Mr. Smee. Everyone else is known by his or her first name, especially Walt when he ran the company.

and determine if they have the tools they need to provide a satisfying customer or donor experience.

- Train all staff on the values and priorities of our organization, not just their daily tasks.

- If a process, procedure, or tradition interferes with a safe and positive donor/customer relationship, modify it or eliminate it.

- When staff does something new, different, or creative that positively impacts a customer, guest, or donor; reward that behavior and use it as an example for others to follow.

- Finally, reinforce the idea that every guest is a V.I.P., and every employee and volunteer is charged with the responsibility of treating him or her as such.

Everyone Neat and Pretty

The "Disney Look" is an integral part of the company's success. Appearance reinforces all the other messages the company asks cast members to convey to guests. And guests notice.

When they write to the company, guests mention three things they like best about Walt Disney World: "the remarkable cleanliness, the friendly employees, and the outstanding show." As explained in the Disney company's book for new cast members, *Welcome to Walt Disney World, A Cast Member's Handbook*, the company emphasizes that cleanliness "is not just about the lack of trash on the ground." Guests are describing the clean look of Disney's people.

Despite the amusement park owners who told Walt his ideas about cleanliness were "screwy" and would be "economic suicide," he insisted that his park be clean and tidy. As Walt developed his idea for his theme park, he toured amusement parks, gardens, and other tourist destinations, he noticed one thing many had in common. They were dirty. Walt despised the filthy conditions he saw. Trash littered the grounds, and employees seemed to come to work in whatever they happened to be wearing when their shift was to begin.

He wanted to differentiate himself from the dirty, greasy parks that had previously been his only choice of a place to take his daughters on weekends. Walt knew cleanliness was crucial to the success of his theme park. As Sam Gennawey relates in his book *The Disneyland Story*, Walt said, "One of these days I am going to build an amusement park...and it's going to be clean!"

Today the emphasis on cleanliness continues. As a Disney Cast Member Handbook says, "When you play a role you must not only act the part, but look the part. ... Next to friendliness we receive more letters complimenting the neat, well-groomed personal appearance of our cast next to anything else." At Disney's theme parks, tattoos were also forbidden and had to be hidden. Any type of facial hair, or a shaved head, was "out of the question."

As former cast member David Ackert said in his book *Forty Years in a Mousetrap*, "Cast members were expected to be almost superhuman." They were never allowed to eat or drink in front of guests. As he also observed, apparently cast members don't bleed, since Band-Aids were never to be visible to guests. As another cast member, Rich Hamilton, said in his *Disney Magic Ideabook*, "When you are on stage, everything matters...no slouching, and no leaning, that was the number-one rule. Everything had to look good, look friendly. We had to be friendly. And it was a good thing."

Not only is the appearance of each cast member important, but so is the park itself. Disney studies guests to determine how closely trash cans should be spaced so guests will use them rather than throw trash on the ground. As a result, Disney places trash cans about 27 feet apart because that's how far Disney observed guests would go, on average, before they would throw trash on the ground.

There are more than 5,400 trash cans in the parks in Anaheim and Orlando, which does not include trash cans in the resorts or parking lots. Each of the trash cans is also designed to match the area where they are located. The trash cans are so well-themed, you can buy replicas of them in the form of salt-and-pepper shakers in Disney gift shops.

Cleanliness maintains the illusion. Tidiness twinkles. Dirt distracts. Clutter confuses. When we keep our areas neat and clean it makes a difference. As Dennis Snow explains in his book *Lessons from the Mouse*, cleanliness is a large part of Disney's success. Although everyone knows dirty towels and linens need to be cleaned, Disney does not let the dirty laundry stick around too long. If you are in a Disney resort, unlike other hotels, you are not likely to see a cart in the hallway full of soiled linens. At least if you do, the cart won't be there long.

The one thing Disney is praised for most frequently, cleanliness and a well-groomed cast, is something we can all copy and employ today. At Busch Gardens, the company provided disciplinary action for its cast members who chewed gum, ate, or smoke in unauthorized

Because gum is difficult to clean from streets and sidewalks, you cannot buy it in any Disney park. To help keep its parks clean, Disney does not sell the product that would make that task significantly more difficult.

areas (including all guest areas). However, taking extra steps to help guests or look your best was almost always rewarded.

Southwest Airlines, in its May 2016 in-flight magazine, featured employee Edison Bloem. He was praised for his excellent customer service, friendly attitude, and the look of his uniform. In the article, he explained, "I always come to work with clothes pressed and shoes polished." Edison's role at Southwest is stocking planes with food and drinks, a position you might not expect to wear clothes that are clean and neatly pressed. But to Bloem, and to the airline, it makes a difference.

Walt Disney's dedication to cleanliness also teaches something more. It uses lessons learned in one area to be successful in another. The attention to cleanliness came from an unlikely source. Much labor and attention goes into the creation of an animated feature. As the Disney company tells its employees in its manual *Your Role in the Walt Disney World Show*, "The meticulous, painstaking process of Disney animation calls for more than 1,500 hand-painted cels for every minute the film is on the screen. It is a long, costly process that produces one animated feature every three years but one that is unmatched in artistry and craftsmanship." It was the studio's origin in animation that created a culture of detail and sacrifice.

Animators must clean film of dust and debris and each frame must work together with the next. This is the heart of film-making and the key to the theme parks and to all of Disney's success.

Message on Hold

I met the founder and owner of a company who made a small fortune recording messages on hold. Long before phone systems went digital and computers made it easy, he would record music and voice messages that would be customized for your business. If you owned a hotel, for example, when a potential guest would call, they might hear about your latest renovations, the new pillow choices you have, or maybe the new shuttle van with complimentary rides to the airport.

In the background you would hear upbeat, happy music, and maybe the sound of surf and waves if you were a beachfront hotel. The message was yours. While no one likes to be put on hold, at least your customers would hear about your hotel, and maybe something that would entice them to come or return for another stay.

The founder of the message-on-hold company did not get his idea from expensive research and development, or after intense focus group questioning. Rather, he came up with the idea when he called his bank. As the bank placed him on hold the music was just ending and the radio station the bank had piped into the phone system went into commercials. The first commercial was for another bank. His bank was playing ads, probably without knowing it, for its competitor.

The detail of the choice for on-hold music or messages was on no one's checklist. The choice of what to put on hold was probably left up to the manager of the day, or more likely what the person next to the machine chose to play. Had the bank followed Disney's example, it would never have chosen to give part of its messaging to a random source: the radio. This is especially true since every caller would be forced to listen to it before reaching a real, live person.

The person making that decision should think about what is best for the customer, or for the consumer. *Obviously*, doing business with us is better than doing business with anyone else. When we institute a culture of caring for our customer and giving our customer our best, we quickly realize everything we say counts. Customers don't focus on just the messages we want them to receive. They focus on everything that matters to them. Waiting on hold always matters to the customer or donor.

If we think being creative or different costs customers, rather than gaining them, consider the choices made by the National Discount Brokers Group around the year 2000. Brokerage offices are not known for a sense of humor or for being non-traditional, but this organization lit up the early internet with one of the first viral sensations.

If you called the National Discount Brokers 800-number you would hear the standard options, but with a twist. Callers would be told they could press 1 to make a trade, press 2 to open a new account, and so on. If you continued listening, choice 7 would be, "To hear a duck quack, press 7." The brokerage company, whose mascot was a mallard duck, received 2 million calls a week. While the flood of calls cost the brokerage company $10,000 a day, *The New York Times* reported that the brokerage had an increase of 75% in new account openings.

Someday My Prints Will Come

For many of us, our business cards and brochures are our first impression with potential donors and customers, but few of us realize the importance these have. What does our business card say about us? Is it easy to read? A business card is not the place to load mission statements, multiple addresses, or bullet points about what we do.

A business card has only one purpose: make it easy for people to reach you. Is there a fax number on our cards? If we have not received a fax within the last 12 months, we should get rid of that number that is taking precious real estate on our card.

Take a fresh look at our business cards and see what it says about us, and what it needs to say. Although business cards are becoming less common, we can apply these techniques to everything we do that is designed to make it easier for people to reach us. Remove all possible barriers to communication and grease the highways.

On with the Show

A generation ago our buildings were our first impression. If you drive around any business park in any town, you can see where fountains used to be or where lush landscaping used to occupy the prime space near the front door. Today, many of those fountains have been filled with flower beds, and in many cases the landscaping has been paved over or choked with weeds. The reason? The internet has become the new first impression. Store fronts are dying.

What does our website say about us? Disney makes its websites clean, fun, and easy to navigate. Whether or not our physical "brick and mortar" building is still visited by customers or donors, it and our website must be warm, welcoming, and geared to serve the needs of our guests, donors, and customers—and no less importantly, our employees.

Recently, Disneyland sold at auction the iconic Disneyland sign that used to greet guests entering the parking lot. Actor John Stamos purchased one side of the sign and agent Richard Kraft purchased the other side. The sign was so iconic and well-designed that people wanted a part of it. Its rumored that Stamos has the large Disney "D" in a prominent place in his backyard. We would do well by designing our first impression so people will not only appreciate it, but want to own part of it.

As we reach out to our customers, clients, donors, and friends, we should look at everything we do as an invitation for them to buy from us, give to our cause, or simply do business with us. As we do, and as we look at things from their perspectives, our buildings, messages, and printed and web material will all work together to help people find us, and make it enjoyable and easy for them to partner with us.

CHAPTER FOUR

Once Upon a Dream

With every decision, Walt would wonder, and ask his employees to consider, how the customer would perceive the results of that decision. He knew the danger of thinking *for* the customer, rather than *of* the customer. The temptation is ever-present to perceive the world from our point of view. It's far too easy to think, "If I like it, then the customer will, too." Walt's desire was to give audiences and guests what they expected, plus a little more.

Weenie Power

Walt Disney was famous for always telling his artists and imagineers to give guests a "weenie." A weenie, in Walt's world, was a reference to his old brown poodle. He would get the dog to follow him around the house by giving him small pieces of a hot dog. The dog would walk along with Walt because it knew a treat was always around the corner.

Walt filled his theme park with architectural weenies. He wanted guests to be curious about what was just ahead. He wanted people to move through his park, to circulate so they would always have a reason to keep moving to see something new.

In any Disney park there are few straight lines. Almost every sidewalk and street has curves. Walt famously designed arching sidewalks and paths so we would be drawn to see what was around the next bend. To help guests move through his park, while also giving them a sense of comfort, he also created anchors that also served as weenies.

The castle, the Matterhorn, Splash Mountain, and Space Mountain can all be see from the road as you approach Disneyland. Even before you enter the park, you have a sense of where things are. It's difficult to get lost in a Disney park, because all lands have sidewalks pointing to the castle, which can be seen from almost every spot in the park. This is not by accident. Even a guest who has never been to Disneyland can become oriented almost instantly because of the elevated, recognizable landmarks in each land. If a guest ever needs to find the way, he or she just needs to look up and check the landmarks.

As we walk to the castle or Space Mountain, there will never be a straight line. But we will never feel lost. Perhaps without even realizing it, we can find our way simply by following the purposely-placed icons. Along the way we will follow gently curving sidewalks, and maybe find other weenies that pull us in different directions, but that is part of the fun.

It would be easier and less expensive to install flower beds and pour concrete in straight lines, but Disney knew a little extra effort up front would pay dividends for years. We may never notice that we all walk a little faster in a Disney park, propelled by the curiosity of what was just around the bend, but Disney knew this would be important to the success of his theme parks.

Like Walt, all of our actions should have donors and guests looking forward to what's next. We need to give our guests weenies. At the same time, we should position those weenies among familiar landmarks along the way, so guests feel safe enough to explore new lands as they unleash their curiosity. Everything we do should end with a tease of something new just ahead. Each sale should end with a coupon or invitation to visit again soon when new clothes will arrive, or a new dish will be offered. In sum, give our customers a familiar landscape, but fill it with weenies and promises of future, curious delights just around the corner. If they liked what they found today, they will love what they discover tomorrow.

Subtle Strength

Part of the magic of Walt Disney is the way he and his company used every available device to tell a story. In Disneyland, Walt wanted to make use of as many resources as possible to immerse his guests in the story he was telling. Not only did the grand settings, the castle, the buildings, and the streets have to convey the story, but so did the costumes, the furniture, and every detail.

Some of the most remarkable immersive details are in areas few guests will notice on first pass. Part of the richness of the visit is discovering the finer points of the story which is unfolding around you. There is always something fun to find on a return trip.

At Walt Disney World and Disneyland:

- The *Lady and the Tramp*-themed-restaurant in Town Square has paw prints in the concrete sidewalk out front.

- The telegraph at the train station in Frontierland spells out Walt Disney's speech from opening day at Disneyland.

- Pick up the telephone in the Emporium and listen to discover you are on a "party line" call which was common for the era.

- Hotel rooms have two peepholes: one at adult height and the other at a child's height.

- The tree farm and solar farm are in the shape of Mickey's familiar silhouette when seen from the air.

Attention to story has been used in other theme parks as well. If you ride the Amazing Spiderman Attraction at Universal's Islands of Adventure, you may notice a phone number on a theater marquee you pass on the ride. The phone number is (407) 224-1783. If you call the number you will hear a recorded message from the theater manager that the theater is closed due to the "recent unpleasantness" caused by Doc Ock. All of these little touches add to a greater experience. We should look for ways to add details and experiences our guests, clients, and donors can discover that may not be immediately obvious.

While it is crucial that we get the "big things" correct in our worlds, there is much that can be gained by flushing out the story, filling all corners with minor details and hidden surprises that our donors or customers will appreciate. It can be as simple as including a soft cleaning cloth when we sell a watch, or an extra dessert at a ball or gala. Always look for ways to add to our narrative and tell it in ways that show we are dedicated to our story.

Good Humor

As we live our story, add humor where appropriate. Give our customers and donors a smile. On Walt Disney World's Splash Mountain, one of the gophers in the attraction pops up and shouts "Go FSU" in honor of one of the designer's alma mater, Florida State University (apparently no Imagineers from the University of Florida were available when Splash Mountain was built). In the Haunted Mansion, at the end of the graveyard scene, which is also the final set piece in the attraction, you will notice a ghostly, rotund lady wearing a Viking helmet singing loudly. The reason? Because the ride is not over until the fat lady sings. Always look for opportunities to fascinate and impress your customers and donors, and if possible include humor.

As stated in a Disney cast member handbook *The Magic is You*, "While we take ourselves seriously, we don't take ourselves too seriously. We try to keep our sense of humor, especially on a tougher-than-usual day." When Marc Davis designed the jail scene at the end of the Pirates of the Caribbean, where the pirates are trying to get the keys from the dog, he added a definite sense of humor. Just feet away, the jail cell door next to them is open.

This is an example of how Marc Davis' sense of playfulness toned down a horrible scene by his addition of humor. After all, the pirates are in jail for presumably doing terrible things. As the lyrics in the song suggest, they have been pillaging, plundering, kidnapping, sacking, and burning the city. They are "really a fright." And now they are about to be burned alive. Disney took the absurdity of making pirates likable and sympathetic by presenting their story with humor and flair.

As you wait to board your boat in the Orlando version of Pirates, there is a dungeon scene where two pirates are playing chess. The scene originally called for two pirate skeletons to be chained to the wall. Deeming this too frightening, the Disney imagineers instead posed the skeletal pair over a table playing chess. Mix scary with fun. If you look closely at the chess game, you will see neither side can win. It's an eternal stalemate.

Honor Each Other

The tombstones you see as you enter the Haunted Mansion are real. Well, they are not real as if there are bodies buried beneath them, but they are real in the sense that the names on them represent real people: Disney cast members. For example, one prominent tombstone reads, "Master Gracey laid to rest, no mourning please at his request." This tombstone honors Yale Gracey who designed many of the special effects within the Haunted Mansion.

In Orlando, the tombstone for Madame Leota honors Leota Toombs who was a Disney model builder. The face floating in the crystal balls in the Haunted Mansion is also Toombs. The voice you hear as you see the crystal ball is that of Eleanor Audley who provided the voice of the wicked stepmother and villain Maleficent in *Sleeping Beauty*. Toombs also appears as the little figurine near the end of the attraction encouraging guests to "hurry back" and "be sure to bring your death certificate." These little details (and laughs) are small additions that add up to a better guest experience.

Along Main Street, U.S.A. you will see many of the windows have fanciful business names on them. The ultimate honor for a Disney cast member is to have his or her name added to a Main Street window. The business and title associated with the cast member usually reflects the employee's contribution to the company. Frank Wells, who was president and chief operating officer under Michael Eisner, was honored posthumously with a window indicating he was the president of Seven Summits Expeditions. He died in a helicopter crash when he was 62 while still actively working for the company. His goal was to climb the highest peak on each of the seven continents, which is memorialized on his Main Street window.

As you walk through the Disney parks, or listen to place names in Disney movies, look for patterns and watch for stories. Almost every name has a purpose or a reason, and often it is to honor or memorialize a cast member. In the same way, we should look for ways to honor our customers, donors, and guests, as well as our fellow employees and staff members.

Give Your Best Customers Something Extra

As Walt Disney was preparing for his company's participation in the 1964 World's Fair, he noticed something about the major corporate sponsors. Each of their pavilions featured a lounge for visiting executives and important guests. It was a place where corporations could entertain them. They could escape the heat and crowds in a private setting, often with nice views of the pavilion and the surrounding World's Fair.

Walt Disney replicated the idea with his Club 33 in Disneyland. Club 33 is a private, exclusive club in the heart of Disneyland's Magic Kingdom. Membership is restrictive and relatively expensive. Named after its address on Royal Street in New Orleans Square, it is located above the Pirates of the Caribbean attraction.

There is no sign for Club 33. If you ring the doorbell to enter you will be asked for your membership number and not allowed in without it. It is the only place in Disneyland where alcohol is served. Its list of features and member benefits is amazing, and more than a few websites are dedicated to rumors and legends about the club and its members.

While every guest at Disneyland is a V.I.P., Walt Disney wanted Club 33 to be the diamond among rubies. He wanted his best customers and closest friends to have a place they could call their own. It was (and is) a special place. Like the corporate lounges at the World's Fair, Club 33 is an almost-secret oasis where only the best customers, guests, and friends can go. Those below are not given less. Disney just reserves this treat for those who are closest to the company.

What do we give our best donors, our best guests, and our closest friends? Few guests at Disneyland even know about Club 33. Yet even if everyone knew about it, not many would feel deprived if they learned they could not enter. Disneyland is still a magical place. Club 33 is simply a nod to a select few, to show them appreciation. Notably, those special guests also pay dues and fees for that privilege.

Like Disney, we should be respectful, courteous, and grateful to all our customers and donors. Each should feel appreciated. Yet, for our best customers, we

Valentine's Day is a big day for White Castle and Waffle House restaurants. While unrelated, both food chains offer special Valentine's Day decorations and seating for couples. Both take reservations for that special day that often fill weeks in advance.

should make them feel extra special.

We should visit or call our best customers and donors—for no reason at all. They expect us to call when we want something (more business, another donation, or a favor), but they should also know we respect them regardless of what they are spending at the moment. Call everyone once in a while to just see how they are doing. Send them free samples of things you know they like, or offer them a sneak peek at something special.

We don't have to build a new theme park to entertain them. Just set aside a special place within it. Allow them to enter early or stay late. Give them a reserved seat at events, or a special seat with you one-on-one where you tell them how much you appreciate their business or donation.

If you have not been to an In-n-Out or Chick-fil-A restaurant, stop by to see what they do for special customers. In-n-Out has a secret menu. Anyone can order from it, but you usually don't know about it until you have eaten there a couple times. An employee might suggest a "secret" addition or you might overhear someone ordering something unfamiliar or something clearly not on the menu. People like the secret menu because it gives them a special status. Because they are "in the know," they feel a kinship and belonging with the restaurant and other customers like them.

In the same way, Chick-fil-A offers an app for your cellphone that tracks your purchases and gives you special treats every once in a while. It also sells calendars late in the year at an inexpensive price that come with twelve coupons for free food; one for each month of the following year. While anyone can buy a calendar, they usually sell out quickly. If you are not a regular customer and see when they are available, you may not be able to get one.

Match your customer or donor's loyalty with your respect and admiration. Give to them as they give to you. And if you are in the southwest and happen to be near an In-n-Out, ask for your French fries "animal style." If you are in a Chick-fil-A, don't pay with cash or your credit card, give their app a try.

First Names Only

Walt broke ground in many ways. Many of the things we now take as common in the business world were started by Walt Disney. Today, we usually call fellow employees and supervisors by their first names. That has not always been true.

When Walt started his studio it was different in many ways. Other studios at the time were a hierarchal bureaucracy where heads of studios were given titles such as mogul or titan. Studio chiefs were legendary in their authority and control over the studios they ran. They told stars who to date, who to marry, and what they could eat. Few people could call Louis B. Mayer, "Louie," or Darryl Zanuck, "Darryl," and expect to work the next day, or perhaps ever work again in Hollywood.

Walt insisted his employees call him "Walt." He would commonly say "Mr. Disney" was his father and he was simply Walt. He wanted his employees to be comfortable with one another, so they could concentrate on their work. Today, it is common for nametags to feature only our first names. We want to be approachable and for our customers, donors, and employees to feel comfortable when communicating with us. However, when we address them, like Disney, we should be respectful and call them "Mr.," "Mrs.," or "Ms." Make it easy for guests and donors to relate to us even as we remain respectful to them.

A Ceremony to Remember

Like Disney, we can look for opportunities to make guests and customers feel important. Every day at just about sunset, something magical happens at the Magic Kingdoms in Orlando and in Anaheim. The United States flag is lowered as part of a simple ceremony. Members of Disney security as well as some other Main Street cast members and musicians gather around the flagpole in Town Square to lower the flag.

Someone, sometime in Disney's management noticed something. As the flag was lowered, some people in the crowd would stop walking by and salute the flag or more commonly stand reverently with their hands over their hearts as the flag was respectfully lowered. Often these people would wear baseball caps with military insignia on them. They were veterans.

Today, if you watch the flag ceremony, you will notice the usual complement of Disney cast members, but you will also notice something else. You will see a guest, frequently an older guest, at the center of the ceremony. As the flag reaches the base of the pole, the guest has the place of honor. The security cast member folds the flag and hands it to the guest as they form a line behind the guest and proceed to the backstage area to conclude the ceremony.

Afterward, Disney cast members present the guest with a certificate and lapel pin memorializing his role in the flag ceremony. Often, a Disney photographer captures the event as well.

Banner Moments

Even if that guest (who is often a veteran with his children and grandchildren at the park) spends two weeks and $10,000 at the Disney resort, the one thing everyone will talk about, and everyone will tell their friends, is that grandpa got to be part of the flag ceremony at Walt Disney World.

Dean Gaschler, a beloved, long-time Walt Disney World Main Street U.S.A. cast member, was once approached by a veteran who asked him how the person was selected to participate in the flag ceremony. As Dean recounts in his book *I Led the Parade!*, the veteran explained his daughter was gravely ill and this would likely be her last visit to the Magic Kingdom with him. Although it was not Dean's role to choose the veteran, he knew whose role it was, and after a brief visit backstage, Dean informed the veteran he would be the one to help with the flag ceremony that evening. The veteran later wrote to Dean:

> I was the Honorary Veteran of the Day on December 5, 2005. After the flag was presented to me, an Honor Guardsman announced to the crowd in Town Square in a strong and commanding voice, 'Ladies

and gentlemen, boys and girls, from Pittsburgh, Pennsylvania, Master Sergeant Ed M____, United States Air Force, Retired, Vietnam Era.' The crowd cheered and applauded. I still get chills when I remember this moment.

Allowing guests to participate in the flag ceremony costs Disney pennies. It is the price of a certificate and lapel pin. Yet, the memories, the nostalgia, and the priceless moment will resonate in far more than good feelings. That veteran and his family will return to the Magic Kingdom. Perhaps what was a single vacation will become an annual ritual. He may never lower the flag again, but will always want to return to the post where he did. On the next visit to the Magic Kingdom, he may even bring more family, friends, and neighbors. And the people who watch the ceremony appreciate it as well, even if they are never chosen to be part of it.

Following Disney's example, I used the official flagpole at the University of the South when I was the director of Planned Giving for the university. We asked the talented and creative folks at Print Services to create a simple, but elegant certificate that said the accompanying flag was flown over the University of the South to honor ____ on a certain date.

We would then ask our vice-chancellor (who serves as president of the university) and our provost to sign it in printed signature blocks at the foot of the certificate. When a donor made a particularly worthy gift (not necessarily a large one), we would buy a brand new United States flag, respectfully raise it to the top of the University's flagpole, then lower it, carefully fold it, and present it to the donor at an appropriate time along with the certificate.

Although it was my idea to begin this at the university, you may wonder, as I did, if it makes a difference. It does.

The first person I presented the flag to was a Vietnam veteran. We happened to fly the flag for him on Veterans Day. He was a relatively young man and I was shocked to learn he died unexpectedly about 8 months after we presented him the flag. He happened to be a generous donor.

When I attended the funeral, the family was eager to meet me. They had read the letters and emails I had shared with him, but more importantly, they had seen the flag certificate and cover letter I mailed him describing our thanks for his gift—and why we sent him the flag. The family had made that flag, and the university certificate with it, the central focal point on a table with some photos, art, and other memorabilia of the veteran's life at the reception following the funeral.

Our little certificate that was dreamed up after thinking about how Disney does it had a profound impact on him *and* his family. It meant a lot to him. On a practical level, it also made estate administration a lot easier. The family did not see the university as some unknown suitor seeking a portion of the donor's estate. Instead, the family saw us as the friend we were.

We were always friends, but the flag and the certificate gave physical proof the relationship was not one way. Yes, the veteran gave generously to the university in life and in his planned gift following his death, but the university gave that love back to him. We continued giving out flags and never regretted the $19 investment we paid for each new flag.

If you want to, as Disney Imagineers do, "plus it," combine the gift of your flag with one from your state capitol or from the United States Capitol. The federal government has an official flag program and most states do as well. Contact your local representative or senator for information on how you can have a flag flown in someone's honor. It is easier than you might think. To be really cool and over the top, take the flag you receive from Washington and fly it at your charity or corporation. Give the flag double duty and double significance.

While the rewards are emotional, and worth it, just for the sentiment and gratitude you will receive from donors or customers, there is a practical effect as well. No customer will stop buying and no donor will stop giving when he or she has been given such a unique and special gift from you. He may never fly the flag or even look at it again. However, he will know you went out of the way to give something no one else could give. There is nothing neater or more "Disney" than that.

The flag is only one example. If you look and are creative, you can think like Disney and find unlimited ways of honoring your donors and customers. All we need to do is stop doing things the old way and start looking at things the Disney way.

Guest Watching

Walt Disney loved watching his guests. Are we watching ours? The companies, organizations, and charities that fail largely do so for one reason: they ignore customers and guests. The most common complaint from donors is that a charity took their money and it was never heard from again. No "thank you," no "how are you doing," no nothing. Interact with donors and customers. Do more than take money.

In the same way, customers expect the businesses they interact with to respect them. Now more than ever, customers have choices where they spend money. There are few monopolies left. Maybe there was once a time when businesses could take their customers for granted. If that time ever existed, it is clearly over.

Most organizations and corporations still act as though customers will always be there and always return. That's good news for us, because if we treat customers well, they will flock to us and abandon those corporations and organizations who don't treat them well. If we watch our customers and donors, we can easily find ways to let them know we care, if we approach it with a little creativity in mind.

On the nonprofit side, for example, we noticed (because we purposefully set out to look for ideas) that some of our donors were passionate about the symphony at the university. We presented one philanthropist who had sponsored a symphony with the conductor's baton from the sponsored performance, signed by the guest celebrity conductor, at a reception following the concert. It was a used little stick of wood, not much more than a chopstick with a grip on the end. The donor loved it. I have no idea where you would even buy a baton or how much they cost, but we

> **Get out of the office: "For God's sake, don't eat off the lot. Stay there... lunch with the guests... talk with them."**
> **—Walt Disney**

gave one away and the donor liked it. We did it again with another donor who supported the orchestra for another performance.

Stories Make Memories

Even if someone spends a thousand dollars a day at a Disney park and stays for two weeks, sparing no expense, experiencing everything the resort has to offer, eventually, no matter how good it is, it will end. The vacation of a lifetime soon becomes a memory among many memories. Disney has to create magical moments so guests will raise those memories above others in their storehouse of cherished moments.

Disney does this by wrapping as much of the experience in a story as possible. We remember stories. Big Thunder Mountain is not a roller coaster. It is a runaway mine train in an abandoned Gold Rush town. The Pirates of the Caribbean tells the story of pirates landing and then looting and burning a Caribbean town. Even the hotels tell stories. The Polynesian, Grand Floridian, and Contemporary are all themed. Every restaurant, lobby, pool, plate, and napkin fits into the story of the resort.

Before Walt Disney World was built, a portion of the property, on what is now Bay Lake, was a hunting and fishing camp. At some point someone at the camp had leaned a lawn mower (the old-fashioned kind that has no engine, but has blades mounted between rotating wheels) against a pine tree. The tree eventually grew around the mower, consuming it.

Disney never misses an opportunity to tell a story. Rather than remove the tree and the old lawn mower, Disney Imagineers left it in place, then created a sign and erected it next to the tree. It reads: "The Lawn Mower Tree, Too long did Billy Bowlegs park his reel slow mower alas, one warm and sunny day aside a real fast grower." To take the story one level deeper, "Billy Bowlegs" was a famous Seminole Indian chief, whose name would be immediately recognizable to anyone aware of Florida history, or who would be inspired enough to look. Where some would see an eyesore, Disney saw a story. Find your stories in places others overlook. Tell your stories and give them life and depth that others will appreciate. Give your guests memorable stories and they will remember you.

Great Housekeeping

You might think the creative ideas at Disney come from a room in a corner office somewhere. All the really neat ideas and decisions spring from some really cool people whose only job is to think up neat ideas. While it is true there are many types at Disney Imagineering that might fit that description, Disney is astute enough to also listen to employees, and even to cast members you might never expect to have or share creative ideas.

If there is one area in the hospitality business that receives the least amount of praise or even attention, it is probably the housekeeping staff who clean hotel rooms. Walt Disney World has more than 25,000 hotel rooms on property, with thousands of housekeeping cast members to keep them clean.

Some of the housekeeping staff at the resort would find stuffed Disney characters left on the floors of rooms and other assorted messes as children and parents would rush each day from the room to experience the Disney parks. Housekeeping hosts began picking them up. Rather than place them on a bed or dresser, they creatively arranged them in the room as a surprise for the children when they returned.

One housekeeping host created a rope ladder out of towels and had the stuffed friends posed in a way that showed they were trying to climb the curtain to see what was going on outside. Others were propped in a circle on one of the beds around a make-believe campfire also made with carefully folded towels. Without invading privacy, housekeeping hosts were finding ways of "plussing" the guest experience.

These unseen cast members were giving children a delight. The children's characters were magically coming to life. It took maybe a little extra time and laundry, but the housekeeping hosts created moments and memories that will be talked about for years. Families now look forward to seeing what surprises might await them in their rooms.

In many hotel operations, where each room is supposed to be cleaned in a certain way and in a certain time period, housekeeping hosts might risk punishment for using extra towels or by picking up "too much" after a sloppy guest (especially those annoying children).

But at Disney, such behavior is rewarded and encouraged. Most hotel managers probably would not appreciate housekeeping hosts deviating from cleaning duties, even a little. But Disney managers know better. They listened. They listened to their staff and they listened as guests at restaurants talked about what they discovered in their rooms when they would return from their day's adventure.

As you set out to work with donors or customers as Disney does, remember certain behaviors that would probably be frowned upon at least initially, or don't make sense economically, should at least be given a shot if you are truly listening to your donors, customers, guests, and staff.

Tried and True

When planning for Disney World, Walt and his brother Roy thought about what attractions should be put there. Would the park have all new attractions, completely different than its counterpart in Anaheim, or would it be an exact duplicate of the West Coast original? The Disney brothers decided the new park would offer some new attractions such as the Mickey Mouse Revue and Country Bear Jamboree along with familiar rides that East Coast residents had seen on television and always wanted to ride, but would probably never travel to California to see. Walt Disney World would be built to have new and different attractions, but would be filled with the old, familiar ones as well.

In the same way, the biggest movie of all time, which happens to be owned by Disney, is *Star Wars: The Force Awakens*. It's no surprise that the story of the movie looks amazingly similar to the first *Star Wars* movie ever made, *A New Hope*. Like its 1977 predecessor, *The Force Awakens* tells the story of a young loner on a forgotten desert planet who has vast unknown potential. She encounters a small robot that contains the secret to destroying a new, massive, sphere-like weapon capable of doing unimaginable harm.

As the good and dark forces race to protect or find the robot, the lead character is quickly whisked to far-away worlds where hints of her power begin to emerge as the good guys figure out the one small vulnerability that will end the threat of what is essentially the third Death Star. *The Force Awakens*, like *A New Hope*, ends with a fleet of starships bombarding the space station while a small group of heroes work inside it to disable its shields. (And my apologies for spoiling the movie, but a key figure dies in the effort to destroy the space station, similar to what happened in the first movie.)

The Force Awakens deserves all the praise and revenue it has received. It is a great movie. However, like so many attractions before it, the magic is not in creating something entirely new, but giving viewers a heaping helping of familiar fun, with a few new added twists and characters.

Taking the familiar and adding slightly to it is a Disney tradition. Disney's first full-length animated picture was *Snow White* (1937). The story behind *Snow White* had been around for centuries. Several European traditions tell the story in different ways, but when Walt released his animated version, the story itself was not new and the characters were familiar to viewers. Disney did not create Snow White, but he did make the character more attractive to modern viewers.

The European tales of Snow White are far darker than Disney's version. As scary as Disney's movie is, it pales compared to European traditions. In folklore, the evil stepmother hired a huntsman to find Snow White and bring back her lungs and liver so she could eat them. Also left out from the Disney version are the poisoned comb and lace bodice (that strangles Snow White). The folk tale also ends with the evil stepmother being exposed. She is presented with iron shoes pulled from a fire that she is forced to wear and dance in until she dies.

As we strive to give our donors, guests, and customers our best, we always achieve more by adding the familiar to anything new we offer. When we wish to try something new, we can follow Walt Disney's lead by coupling the new thing with an abundance of familiar material. Our guests expect new and novel, but they want it in the context of the familiar.

Walt's Waltz

Disney Imagineer Marty Sklar, in his book *One Little Spark*, points out that for many of us, recalling an image of a Disney movie is not an image at all. It's music; a song. While many of Walt Disney's most memorable musical scores are original, some are not. In *Sleeping Beauty* (1959), Disney used a ballet composed by Peter Ilyich Tchaikovsky in 1889. The studio added lyrics to the ballet's memorable motif and a musical number was born. Disney took the familiar story of "Sleeping Beauty," added the well-known music of Tchaikovsky, and gave both new life.

Walt Disney had an unsurpassed ability to sense what people liked about the familiar and blend just enough "new" to make it attractive and not passé. As we reach out to donors, customers, and buyers, we can follow his lead. We must avoid the temptation to always be creating something new; or worse: to simply do the same old thing again. New is wonderful and exciting, but there are fewer new things out there than we may realize. As we entice and attract people to our organization or cause, give them new, but be certain that there is plenty of familiar in the package as well.

CHAPTER FIVE

The Personal Touch

A Way of Life

Walt Disney was fond of saying, "The personal touch is a way of life." He coupled that philosophy with the idea, "Every guest is a V.I.P.; if there is no audience, there is no show." At Disney, if you don't believe these two philosophies, the company does not hide its belief that you may not be a good fit in the organization. For us, too, the personal touch is a way of our life, and whether we sell a product, provide a service, or seek donations for a cause, the personal touch is crucial.

Playwright Sean O'Casey once said, "All the world's a stage." Walt Disney could have said the same thing. Only he took this concept to its logical conclusion. If you work for Disney, you are not an employee or staff, you are a cast member. You are part of the show. If you work where guests can see you, you are on stage. If you work or go where guests cannot see you, you are off stage, or backstage. It's always part of the show.

It's All Personal

One of the worst clichés ever introduced into the English language is the phrase, "Don't take it personally." As human beings, everything is personal all the time. Nothing is ever not personal. Of course, the saying evolved as an attempt to lessen the pain of something that was about to be said: "Don't take this personally, but…" You know the words that follow will not be pleasant. If the negative outcome would happen to everyone in your situation, and not just you, then surely it must hurt less. At least that's what those words imply. How ridiculous.

Somehow, somewhere, somebody told someone else something terrible preceded by the words, "But don't take it personally," as if that would make everything better. What is not said, but certainly implied, is that, "We say that to everyone like you." Bad news is bad news. The fact that you are the 124th person today to hear it does not make it any better. The fact that others share the same pain does not mean yours hurts any less.

When we tell someone not to take something personally, we strip them of their dignity, importance, and humanity. While the words may say, "this happens to everyone," the message to the one hearing it is you are no longer a person. You are a statistic.

Disney understands how intensely personal all interactions are. In its corporate training literature, the company reminds its cast members, "Just remember…one personal experience, good or bad, usually makes the greatest impression. The personal touch is a way of life…a vital ingredient in the success of our show."

Walt Disney insisted *everything*

Never should we ever tell a donor, guest, or customer to not take something personally. It's all personal. *Always*.

is personal. Cast members at the Disney parks are trained to treat every guest like a V.I.P. While tens of thousands of people will be in the park that day, each one should feel as though the park was made just for them.

While crowds tend to make this difficult, the staff usually more than makes up for it. Each cast member is instructed to answer every question with respect. Disney tells cast members, "Our guests may not always be right, but they will always be our guests." Former cast member Jim Cunningham recalls, as quoted in Dennis Snow's book, *Lessons from the Mouse*, "The guests may not always be right, but let's allow them to be wrong with dignity."

Even if a cast member has been asked ten times in the last five minutes what time the three o'clock parade begins, they're instructed and encouraged to smile and answer the question for the guest as if that guest was the only one they would encounter that day. How could we expect a guest to know someone else had just asked the same question? As a Disney cast member guidebook states, "You may be asked the same question time after time...but remember for each guest, *it's the first time.*"

The Disney company explains in its cast member handbook: "We may entertain 100,000 guests in a single day, but we do everything possible to entertain them one at a time." Disney management encourages cast members to take time to interact with guests, answer questions, talk, and joke with their guests.

Disney encourages its cast members to seek out ways of making each guest's visit special. Cast members should volunteer to help families take photos, rather than wait to be asked. Think of how many vacation photos are missing a family member because that person took the picture. At Disney, all photos should include all family members.

Every visitor is to be treated as if he or she were the only visitor that day. Even security hosts can get in on the act in unexpected ways. As Dennis Snow explains in *Lessons from the Mouse*, it is not uncommon for a Disney security host to stop an unsuspecting child and issue the youngster a citation for having the "biggest smile of the day."

When we encounter donors, guests, and customers, we are often asked the same questions repeatedly. While it can be frustrating to be asked a couple dozen times where the food is, or where the silent auction is, the would-be donor asking does not necessarily know we have been asked that question before. Disney insists its cast members rise above the urge to roll eyes or give a quick answer. Each guest is entitled to the same courteous and full response. It is as if it were the best question ever asked and we were born to answer it.

While we may all see the same movie, or ride the same attraction, we all view it from slightly different angles, and it affects us in different ways. While everyone may cry when Old Yeller dies, we do so for unique reasons. Maybe it is because we identify with young Travis and his love for the dog. Maybe it is we because we love dogs and hate to see the tragic events unfold. It could be the person next to us is crying and we join in sympathy. More likely it is a combination of these. Even so, how Old Yeller's death affects each of us is as unique as we are.

Don't Let Small Problems Become Big Ones

Just as every guest is an individual, so too should be the way we handle their problems, individually. The solution is unique to the guest and the situation. And most important of all, Disney has a culture of handling problems before they become too large. Disney trains its cast members to handle little problems while they are still little. While the rules are important to Disney, the rule of keeping the customer happy usually beats all others.

If we wait to handle something, problems usually do not go away on their own. Rather, they tend to grow, and the person with the problem almost always tells as many people as they can about it. Little problems that become big problems are more difficult to resolve. Disney knows this and spends much of its time and attention resolving small problems while they are still relatively easy to handle. Disney empowers cast members to take all reasonable and appropriate steps to solve small problems so they don't have an opportunity to grow larger.

Suppose you are in a Disney resort lobby and watch as an angry man approaches the front desk. He tells the cast member he is upset. He just checked in, opened the window, and saw the hotel pool under construction. He reserved the room months ago specifically for the pool view and what he had so looked forward to was now a construction site. The reaction by almost any other front desk clerk would probably be something

Unlike wine, problems don't get better with age.

like, "I am sorry, but the pool is down for maintenance and it's just unfortunate that it's at a time when you are here. Please don't take it personally."

A Disney cast member would probably respond differently. Assuming, for this example, there are no other rooms available with a view of another pool, a Disney clerk would respond with empathy rather than a lecture about how "maintenance happens." Disney empowers its cast members to find innovative solutions.

The clerk might leave a beach bucket, sunscreen, and a Disney beach towel in the family's room with a note signed by the staff about how much they regret the vacation's timing. The note might go on to give them a discount or other token of esteem to help ease the disappointment and ideally encourage them to return and use the gifts when the pool reopens. Disney encourages its cast members to see problems as guests see them, and to respond from the guest's point of view.

Perhaps the most striking result of how personally the Disney Company treats its employees is Walt Disney World itself. The resort in Orlando was always going to be called Disney World. After Walt's death in 1966 (five years before the park's opening), Walt's brother Roy was tasked with completing the Florida Project. As Disney World was about to open, he changed the name to Walt Disney World so people would always remember the man behind the name.

In Your Eyes

Walt Disney was famous for walking through Disneyland at all hours. He wanted to see the park from his guests' point of view. If he only walked through the park when it was empty, he could not appreciate all the things his guests could teach him about his theme park.

Perhaps, more than any other talent Walt Disney had, was his ability to see the world from other points of view. When he visualized and planned a movie, from the beginning, he looked at it as a finished product from the audience's point of view. When he planned a theme park, he could visualize all the details, almost to the point where he could see items on gift shop shelves. He thought about how people would experience the things he designed.

As he paced the raw acreage that would become Disneyland, he would take visitors on a tour of the future park with a guide's precision showing where everything would be. Although the park existed only on paper, it was real to him. Designer John Hench said, "[Walt Disney] pointed out Main Street, Fantasyland, and other nonexistent features." As detailed in the Disney Institute's book *Be Our Guest, Perfecting the Art of Customer Service*, Walt Disney believed in his park so much, it was real long before it was constructed.

Imagineer John Hench also observed, as recounted in Todd James Pierce's book, *Three Years in Wonderland*, that Walt would often "...crouch down so he could see how the fantasy environment would appear from a child's point of view. Inside his mind he would shift the buildings, widen and then narrow walkways.

I remember several Sundays seeing Walt across the street...stepping things off in the weed-filled lot, standing, visualizing, all by himself." He wanted to know what his guests would see and feel as they visited his park.

Living Target

Bad things happen when we fail to appreciate the point of view of our customer. One day as I was sitting down to eat with my family, the phone rang. The caller was a pleasant young woman calling from a charity I had contributed to in the past. She informed me she was calling to let me know about all the improvements the charity was making to its facilities.

I told her I appreciated her call, but her time would be better spent on someone else. I explained I was a professional fundraiser, and taught customer relations and fundraising, and knew why she was calling (to raise money) and knew many people in the charity's advancement office. If I wanted to give, I knew who to call.

She assured me she was not calling for money and just wanted to give me an update. Reluctantly, I listened knowing what train would soon be coming down the now-promised, non-fundraising tracks. For about ten minutes that seemed an eternity, she ran through a script telling me about the updates. At the end her pace slowed and she capped the narrative, "Of course, this cannot happen without you." She then let me know they had "targeted me" for a gift of $500.

The first thing I did was cover the phone and tell my wife, "We've made it." I could not believe the charity would suspect or expect me to make such a gift on the spur of the moment. Apparently, they knew something about my income and finances I did not know. After a brief pause, I told her I could not make such a gift, but I was interested in making a planned gift. I asked if she could have someone call me with more information. She said she would.

A planned gift is a will, trust, or other type of gift that takes a little planning, but often results in large gifts. The average phonathon gift is probably in the neighborhood of $50–$100, while the average planned gift is around $50,000. However, she was not watching her guest. She was watching her script. She was charged with getting $500 from me, and nothing else, or more precisely, *nothing more.*

Although I saw her role as a fundraiser, she saw her role as a caller who was trying for a specific target. Nonetheless, her promise to have someone call me with more information about making a planned gift was made ten years ago. I have a feeling the call will never come. Had she thought about her true reason for calling, and not simply to achieve or come close to the targeted amount, she could have potentially scored much more.

In the decade since then, the fundraising staff there has probably turned over a couple of times, and the young lady hired for the phonathon is likely long gone. But things have changed at that charity. Recently I was giving a webinar where about seven hundred people attended. I did not go over the attendance list but was told later how many people listened to it.

About a week after the webinar, I received a hand-written notecard. It was from a manager at the charity. She thanked me for the webinar and complimented me on several key points I had made. She then had several other folks at the non-profit write additional messages and notes to me. Receiving that unexpected, highly personal, sincere note lifted me for days, and greatly increased the probability of me giving to the charity more often and more abundantly.

Each guest is an individual. For us, each person we contact is unique, even if they are the twentieth person we have contacted that night. No matter what side of any relationship we are in, and no matter how much we know the other side, when we remember we are dealing with an individual, and treat the person accordingly, everything goes better. To Disney, and to us, everyone we come in contact with is a V.I.P.

Secret to Service

Walt Disney always coached his cast members that they served guests, but were not servants. As explained in the Walt Disney Company's 1987 cast member guide, *Your Role in the Walt Disney World Show,* "Always keep your head held high, with your eyes focused before you. With downcast eyes, you place yourself in a position of servant to other people. ...The guests in the park are your guests, and though you are there to assist them, they do not own you."

In addition, Walt Disney always reminded cast members to keep it simple. "Actually, there are no real secrets to being a Disney 'people expert,' but there are a number of important things that are musts in the script. ... Practice a friendly smile.... We use friendly courteous phrases such as 'please,' 'thank you,' and 'enjoy the rest of your stay.'"

In the same handbook, Disney reminds its cast members that smiling and friendly phrases go together. They cannot be separated. Walt Disney said the results come naturally. "You will be pleasantly surprised how well our internal friendliness among our cast members leads to an even greater external friendliness with our guests." And as the Disney Cast Member manual reminds employees today: "You are now part of the World's Most Spectacular Show."

Walt wanted an immersive experience for his guests. He wanted them to forget about the outside world and be lost in his. He did not want anything to ruin the fantasy. There are no security guards at Disney; instead, there are security hosts and hostesses. Disney has no rides; it has adventures, shows, and attractions.

The same standards that Walt Disney applied then, and the company still applies today, work for anyone wanting to make a good impression. Anything in our mannerisms or appearance that distracts should be abandoned. When we work with a customer or donor, we don't want them to remember how "unique" our tattoo was or how we ate all the candy in the coffee table dish bowl.

Disney cast members have a bounce in their step and should always have a genuine smile. As one Disney expert, Tom Skaggs, says in *Be Our Guest*, "...one of the things that most sets Disney apart is our cast—and it's their special, individualized, and unscripted interactions with guests that create the most memorable Disney moments."

The company encourages cast members to seek guest contact and to display appropriate body language at all times. If you ask them for directions, they will either show you where you want to go by walking you there, or if they do motion with their hand, they will use two or more fingers, never just their index finger. All cast members are trained to point courteously. At another leading theme park in central Florida, Busch Gardens, its 1980s-era cast member handbook states: "'You're on stage' is an important slogan at Busch Gardens. You will never have a second chance to make a good first impression."

Regardless of where a Disney cast member works, they are always "on stage" any time they are in a public area. Disney asks its cast members: "Imagine yourself as a guest bringing your family to the Walt Disney World Resort, and as you walk down Main Street a Disney character is sitting at a table talking with a co-worker over a cup of coffee and a cigarette. Doesn't sound like Disney, does it?"

Recently, I talked with a client in Alaska who had never been to a Disney park. He was middle-aged and had never had a chance to visit. However, he had just returned from his first trip to Disneyland in California and was excited to talk with me about it. When I asked him what it was like, he told me he kept asking the cast members how they did it. He wanted to know why they were all so friendly and helpful. He did not talk about the new attractions or new shows, or all the money the company has spent updating and rehabilitating attractions. He was fascinated by the employees.

Walt Disney knew his cast members were vital to the success of Disneyland. When you ask guests what was special about their visit, it is almost always a cast member they mention. *The Wall Street Journal* on March 18, 1975 (as quoted in *Your Role in the Show*), stated: "...all the people waiting on you are so friendly, and everywhere you look, on hundreds of acres of land, there is not a speck of litter, that you just let the orderliness of it all wash over you. Someone is taking care of you."

We, too, can take care of the ones we serve. No matter what product, service, or mission we have, it is our people, and the attitude of our people, that matter.

An Audience of One

Walt Disney always saw his customers as guests. A family in a movie theater or a family heading to Disneyland was not a customer, and certainly not a number. It was a group of individuals. In a very real sense, Disneyland was Walt's home and when you came to this Magic Kingdom, you were literally entering a place where Walt *lived*.

As you enter the Magic Kingdom in Disneyland, and walk down Main Street, U.S.A., you will see a fire station to your left. Above it is Walt's apartment. He and his family would stay there. In the window you will notice a small lamp burning. The company and its employees leave this on as tribute to Walt. From this window Walt would watch guests in his park. You were in his home.

> Walt's apartment is still decorated today much as it was then. It is not used much, except for some corporate gatherings. The only major difference between the apartment today and when Walt used it is that it no longer has the fire pole Walt used to slide down to enter the lower floor.

Walt delighted in watching his guests. He wanted to see where they went and how they moved from place to place. He was fascinated by what motivated them. He watched guests one at a time, and made mental notes of what appeared important to each.

Walt loved being in his apartment, but liked being in the park even more. He would often don a disguise or simply slide down the fire pole as himself and enter the park to experience it with the people he built it for: his guests. When we love our guests, customers, or donors as much as he did, how can we not be successful?

Anything Your Heart Desires

If you have ever been on Main Street, U.S.A. in the morning, you know a crowd forms waiting for the rest of the Magic Kingdom to open. As you stand among the thousands of people, you hear families and guests discussing strategy. Some talk through a plan, charting the course for the morning, or even the entire day.

The more dedicated souls have a park map they have been working on for weeks. Many are complete with highlighting, pre-drawn stops for meals, and even restroom breaks. Although you will hear dozens of conversations, you will not hear anyone say, "Let's wait and see where they want us to go."

The guests waiting to see the Magic Kingdom come to the park with their own expectations and their own desires. Even those who are visiting for the first time have read about or heard about some aspect of the park that has drawn them to it. Some may make a dash for Space Mountain. Some go right to Splash Mountain. Others want to see the Jungle Cruise right away. Some even continue to mill around Main Street, U.S.A. as others rush toward the depths of the park.

Like guests in a Disney park, customers and donors come to us with their own notions, ideas, and goals. Our priorities are not necessarily their priorities. While they might understand and agree that the new dormitory is important, or the playground badly needs rehabilitation, it is not always what motivates most of them. Too often in non-profit and even for-profit organizations, we make the mistake of looking inward for answers, rather than paying attention to those we serve.

Our board may have discussed the new dormitory for months, or even years. It may have been so contested that some friendships were strained or some board members resigned. All movement has a cost. Yet, to most donors, that is unimportant.

While the donor might agree a new dorm is badly needed, the donor sees the campus from a different perspective than the board and staff. The donor knows that just because a new dorm is being built, the library, cafeteria, and classroom buildings are no less important. A donor with a passion for funding science lab equipment is not suddenly going to stop funding it because we have called and said we are building a new dorm. Yet, at most non-profits, not only do we expect it, we demand it. We cannot force someone who is intent on seeing Adventureland to go to Tomorrowland because it suits our goals better. Our guests will go only where they want to go.

Priority Perspective

We must be careful when identifying institutional priorities that they remain only that: priorities. A priority is one consideration among others. By definition, it is not exclusive. It only means it has more importance than something else. Just because one thing is more important does not diminish the worth of the other thing.

It's easy to forget that what is a priority for us or our institution may be only known to the donor or customer in a passing comment. Even though we spend lots of money on a flashy new webpage dedicated to the latest, greatest need, or equip our gift officers and sales staff with the best talking points; donors and customers still only pay attention to what's important to them. We cannot change this.

Walt Disney was relentless in observing and talking to his guests. He wanted to make sure he offered products, services, and experiences they wanted; not necessarily what was easiest for him to offer. He had no priorities that were not ultimately his guests' priorities.

Move Mountains

The year 1975 was an important one for the Magic Kingdom in Orlando. The theme park was still relatively new, only four years old. One of the first major expansions was the addition of Space Mountain in Tomorrowland. It would be the first thrill ride there. It was a huge addition for the young park and was a milestone in other ways, too. Unlike other attractions that were original to California and brought to Orlando, Space Mountain was built first on the East Coast.

Along with Space Mountain came other Tomorrowland additions and upgrades. StarJets, Carousel of Progress, and the WEDway PeopleMover were all added to the futuristic land. Disney officials rightly predicted an increase in excitement, attendance, and a general "buzz" about their theme park. They were right: the year saw an increase in attendance. Around 12,515,000 guests went to Walt Disney World in 1975, which was up from 10,834,000 the year before. Yet, Disney management also kept one important fact in mind as they watched the turnstiles spin.

People don't come to a Disney park for a singular purpose. They want a total Disney experience. In the same year that Disney spent more than a reported $650 million on all the additions and improvements in Tomorrowland (while also spending money to construct many of the same attractions in Anaheim), Disney continued adding and improving other areas in the Orlando resort unrelated to Tomorrowland.

In 1975, Disney also completed construction of the Lake Buena Vista Shopping Village with 29 shops and four restaurants. It added 60 Treehouse Villas, a new America on Parade celebration of the country's bicentennial, and expanded each monorail train from five cars to six. Even while Disney rightly predicted a surge in interest and enthusiasm for Tomorrowland, it also knew other areas were no less important.

No matter what we do or what we invest, our donors and customers are going to expect us to be well-rounded. If we are updating Mission to the Moon to a become a new attraction called Mission to Mars, our guest may still prefer the Jungle Cruise, has never ridden Mission to the Moon, and has no plans to check out Mission to Mars. No matter how badly we want a donor to fund a particular project, or a customer to buy a particular product, it must always remain one of many choices. Donors will always give where they want to give, not where we want them to give. Customers will buy what they want to buy.

Dead Letter Office

Consider the United States Postal Service. While many of us don't use the mail as much as our parents did, the U.S. Postal Service is a minor miracle. Pretend for a moment that no one ever came up with the idea of mail. If someone were to approach you and say he or she would come to your house six days a week and pick up your letters and deliver them anywhere in the country in a couple of days for just a couple of quarters, you would rightfully call that person crazy. Logistically, it is a near-impossible feat to move so much mail so quickly, so efficiently. The miracle is even greater when the same person tells you that you will also receive mail from other people six days a week.

Yet, the U.S. Postal Service often fails to realize its true purpose. It fails to recognize its strengths and instead exposes its weaknesses to a point where it is almost self-defeating. Case in point is a moment just after the turn of this century when the post office decided it was time for a change.

As reported in the *Chicago Tribune* on March 5, 2007, "Time Stands Still When You Are Waiting in Line at the Post Office," the U.S. Postal Service started "phasing out" clocks in its 37,000 post offices around the country. The postal service said it was removing clocks from all its lobbies as part of a "retail standardization program" to give their lobbies a more uniform appearance.

The post service denied the move was in response to complaints from customers that they were waiting too long in line. Rather, it said, "Clocks are probably not appropriate in the retail environment." It emphasized that it was not forcing the removal, only asking local offices to take away the clocks, because it wanted people to focus on postal *service* and not the clock. Customers did not quite agree with the removal of the clocks from post office lobbies: 90.6% of respondents to a *Chicago Tribune* survey indicated that removing the clocks from waiting areas was a "bad move."

When you think of "postal service," are the images positive? While the postal service insists the move was for the consumer's benefit, the consumer knew better, and newspaper cartoons and columnists chimed in. The suspected reason was service was horrible and the clocks reminded all of us how long we had to wait for the privilege of enduring it.

If you were playing a word association with someone and you were asked to react to the word "post office," most people would not respond with "service" or "customer service." While several books have been written on the innovations and advances at both UPS and Federal Express, no known books exist on the same subject highlighting the logistical miracle that is the post office, which handles more volume than either of its relatively new competitors. Rather, the one extra-curricular product the post office has given us is a new phrase, "going postal." Its meaning is anything but flattering.

The irony is clear. The post office does wonders. Yet, people hate the post office. Ask anyone about the post office and you are likely to get a negative reaction. Ask them about their letter carrier, and you are likely to get a far different response. People generally love the loyal, friendly person who delivers the mail each day.

To see what the post office gets right, and where it could be better, read *The Fred Factor* by Mark Sanborn. You will want to have a letter carrier like the one who delivers mail to Sanborn. Fred is the letter carrier that not only delivers Sanborn his mail, but generally makes life better for the author. If only Fred ran the whole post office, people would be making up reasons to mail things, just so they could deal with people like him.

Perhaps, if the post office thought more about its reason for being, it would concentrate on the people it serves and focus less on whether there is a clock in the lobby. For example, why doesn't the post office have a drive-through? There appears to be only a couple post offices in the United States that offer customers the convenience of a drive-through.

Other countries such as Bahrain embrace the idea of giving their customers a drive-through post office. Although Americans can pick up meals, do their bank transactions, and drop off dry cleaning from the comfort and convenience of their cars, buying stamps or dropping off a package is not in the system, at least for now.

One of the great things about Walt Disney is he did not insist his customers do things his way. He was quick to change his approach to match his guests' desires. Once, chief Disneyland landscaper Bill Evans approached Walt and told him of a problem he was having at the park. He told the boss his beautiful flower bed was being trampled and ruined by the guests. As John Hench recounts in his book *Designing Disney*, Evans asked Walt to put up a fence to keep the guests out.

While he was a horticultural expert, and known for his beautiful landscaping, Evans lost focus. He thought his job was to create elegant landscaping. In reality, his job was to give guests a visual treat; to offer them something beautiful to behold as they walked through the Magic Kingdom. The flowers were there for the guests. Walt told Evans they would not build a fence; instead, they would pave the pathway.

In an amusing story on how Walt cherished entertaining his guests, he had to handle another problem coming from the landscaping department. Just before opening day at Disneyland, there were not enough plants and flowers in the park. Disney landscapers had already purchased and cleaned out all the plant nurseries in Orange County and in many of the neighboring communities. They could not grow plants fast enough and there were none they could buy locally.

Disney, in typical Walt fashion, had Evans go to the Disneyland parking lot and gather some weeds. He then had them planted throughout the park and had Evans put Latin name tags on them. Problem solved. Walt's job (and Disneyland's) was to entertain. And as guests walked by plants that were clearly weeds, but with ostentatious-sounding scientific names, it was worth a chuckle or laugh until real plants could arrive.

Walt Disney knew his business: create an environment that guests will enjoy and appreciate. The mistake the post office makes is an underlying belief they are in the business of moving letters and packages. While that is what they do, it is not why they do it. They move parcels and notes to help people. They do it to make life better. Disney got it. Fred gets it. Why don't Fred's superiors?

Five Singular Sensations

When we are working with customers, donors, or guests, remember that they (and we) all experience our world through the five senses. We should strive to stimulate as many of them as possible. At Walt Disney World, as you walk down Main Street, U.S.A., Disney floods all five of your senses. Nothing is left to chance. Nothing is arbitrary. Everything is carefully calculated to give you a complete experience, where every sense complements the other. What you see amplifies what you hear and smell, and vice-versa.

Disney coordinates this by controlling the illusion of space and size. Along Main Street you encounter buildings where the first story is built almost full size. The second story is a little smaller than normal sized. The third floor is smaller than the second. The floors are progressively shorter.

In practical terms, it allowed Disney to build a three-story building for the cost of a two story building. To the guest, it gives the illusion of height. The guest gets the sense that all the buildings are full sized, and that they are walking down a typical Main Street with normal, three-story buildings. Without even realizing it, you are seeing a "typical" Main Street that is like no other in the world.

At the end of Orlando's Main Street is Cinderella Castle. Although it appears to be made of rock and brick, it is made only of fiberglass covering a sturdy, modern steel frame. At the base of the castle the faux bricks are large. As your eye follows them to the heights of the castle, the builders used increasingly smaller molds for the brickwork. It gives the castle the illusion of being higher and more majestic than it actually is.

The illusion is also as much with what you hear in addition to what you see. As you walk down Main Street, you will hear background music that sounds authentic to the buildings surrounding you. As the setting only represents the past as we remember it (and maybe not as it actually was), so too is the music reminiscent of, and not a recreation of, music of that era.

> According to Disney lore, two characters from the Disney movie *Summer Magic* opened a hat shop on Main Street. It is the one that sells Mickey Mouse hats (and other styles) to guests. The address of the hat shop is 63, acknowledging the 1963 release date of the movie. Look for another reference to the movie on the window of the Emporium.

Commonly heard on the background speakers from the castle to the train station on Main Street are antique-sounding tunes with titles such as "Flitterin'," "Beautiful Beulah," and "Summer Magic."

The music you hear is not from the early 1900s. Rather, it is the more modern creation of the Disney musical duo, the Sherman Brothers. They composed all three songs for the Disney movie *Summer Magic*, starring Burl Ives and released in 1963.

As you stroll down Main Street, the sidewalk is red. The gold leaf on the windows glistens and the buildings sparkle. Your nose is not left out, either;

especially near the bakery, scents of candy and cookie dough are blown directly onto Main Street.

Walt Disney understood we interact with the world through our five senses, and process everything through our memories and experiences. When all five senses work together, our experience is richer and more complete.

Sweet Smell of Success

Realizing the importance of appealing to all the senses, Disney ensures you are immersed in the total experience. The sights, sounds, and smells all set the stage. It's more than a happy coincidence as your mind nostalgically returns to a time in America that never really existed. The smells of cookies and cakes make you want to complete the experience by satisfying your only senses left out, touch and taste. While Disney may not be the first to engage all senses, it is certainly a master. Now others follow Disney's lead.

Although it is not widely publicized, the large, worldwide hotel chains are paying more attention than ever to the total guest experience. When you walk into a lobby, you are being silently, but overwhelmingly branded.

Marriot, Starwood, and Hyatt all use custom scents in their lobbies, halls, and rooms. They use air fresheners to pump scented air and

Scents at Disney are so important and recognizable that one candle company sells a candle with a smoky scent inspired by the "Rome Burning" scene on Spaceship Earth in Epcot.

use carefully chosen and formulated cleaning supplies and soaps. Everything you smell on their properties is by design. The corporations use scents to gently, but affirmatively remind you of the relaxing, exciting, or modern feeling that matches the style of the property and mood of the customer.

The furniture, colors, carpet, desk, and of course, background music are also designed, just like at the Disney parks, to give the customer a complete sensory experience, leaving nothing to chance. When we design our office or our waiting area, or plan a special event, we should take special care that all five senses are accounted for, and control as much as possible the experience each guest will have while with us.

As Kimpton Hotels Chief Operating Officer Niki Leondakis said in an interview in the April 14, 2009, issue of *Travel and Leisure* magazine, "We didn't want guests to be cognizant of the smell...we wanted it to subtly create a memory and evoke the Kimpton experience whenever they walk into the lobby." More than just masking bad smells, modern corporations want an immersive branding experience. The look, sight, and sounds when you are in their presence are all important.

How do we engage the senses? Even if we have no budget, we might want to approach our office space (or car or lobby) with the same care that Disney and these mega-corporations use. Plant flowers near our front door, or use a pleasant air freshener, at a minimum. At the same time get rid of bad or offensive odors. Look at everything as if we were visiting our workspace for the first time and always know that everything brands us. We might as well, as Disney and major hotels have done, control that branding rather than letting it control us.

It costs nothing to have a clean space and a uniform look. Even if we don't want to spend money, simple choices can make a big difference. We don't have to spend any money to have a fresh look at everything we do, and experience it with all five senses—as our customers and donors do. At a minimum, we should see the world through the eyes, ears, and noses of our guests. By considering and controlling (as much as we care to) the guest experience, we begin defining our organization on our terms. We give guests a perception that is purposeful, not unpredictable.

CHAPTER SIX

We Work So Others Play

When Walt Disney designed Disneyland he wanted to shelter guests from the cares of the outside world. He built an earthen berm around the perimeter of the park and planted trees as a living barrier. Once guests were inside the park, they would be fully immersed in Disney's land. They would not be distracted by the sights and sounds of the world they left behind.

While the construction crews and designers set the stage, Walt Disney knew it was his cast members that would complete the illusion. He reminded them of the importance of their roles. He said, "We are open 365 days a year. We work while others play."

While Disney wanted his cast members to enjoy their roles and love their jobs, he also wanted them to know they were always there for the guests. It took their hard work so guests could play. Much of that work would be ensuring that the setting, attractions, and shows, as well as the people who operated them, worked in harmony.

Local Motion

Early on Walt decided Disneyland would have separate themed sections. While the names and ideas evolved in planning, the result was Disneyland would have a Main Street, U.S.A., Tomorrowland, Adventureland, Frontierland, and several more that would be added over the years.

Disneyland was a show and it was important that all parts of the show work together. Walt Disney's cast members did not have jobs, they had "roles" in the show. Accordingly, they acted, not worked. They hosted guests, not served tourists. In the same way an actor on a Broadway show would not stop to take a phone call in the middle of the play, Disney did not and does not want its cast members to break the illusion.

Walt designed Disneyland so cast members could get from one side of the park to the other without guests seeing them. Legend says Walt Disney did not want to see one of Frontierland's cowboys walking through Tomorrowland to get to his post. It would ruin the setting of Tomorrowland.

In the same way that the colors, sights, and sounds of Disneyland matter, Walt knew the success of his theme park depended on attitude, the look and the outlook of his cast members. He was aware that while his park would be filled with attractions, his employees were always going to be the stars.

Look Like Disney

Of utmost importance to the Disney organization is the way cast members look. Since they are cast members, their costumes are a necessary and important part of the show. Backstage, Disney has no uniform section. It has a wardrobe, and cast members are issued costumes. Certainly some of those costumes are familiar cartoon characters, but costumes also include tuxedos, ball gowns, and railroad conductor outfits. Cast members receive their costumes from the world's largest wardrobe. And as Disney tells its cast members, its wardrobe department is larger than all movie studio costume departments combined. No matter what role you have in the Disney show, you will always look well-dressed and ready for the role you play for your guest.

To keep the magic in the proper places, the Disney company built tunnels, called Utilidors, beneath Walt Disney World, so employees could move between lands (and break rooms and supply rooms) without being seen. Cast members can find well-hidden doors which lead them down stairs so they can travel safely below you without being seen and while keeping the illusion above true and consistent.

At Disney, the company invests a lot of money to make sure its cast members have

Walt Disney World actually has no underground tunnels. Most of what you see at the Magic Kingdom was built on top of a hidden, first story of the park. When the Seven Seas Lagoon was created, the earth to create the lake was used to build up the Magic Kingdom. Florida's water table is too high to have a basement or underground structure.

costumes that match their environment. Whether that costume is for a performer on one of the park's many stages, or for a monorail captain, the clothing must look the part, and also be comfortable and functional for the person wearing it.

Disney also insists that clothing be clean, pressed, and free of tatters and tears. Cast members can be disciplined for holes in their clothes, or for not wearing a name tag.

Filling Costumes

While Disney recognized that the "look" of cast members was important, the attitude of the person wearing the costume is no less critical. Just as Disney uses the term cast member rather than employee to describe the people who work for the company, when guests come to the park they expect those cast members to perform their roles in predictable ways.

Before they even work in their positions for the first time, every employee, from custodian to manager, attends a program called Traditions. In Traditions they learn about the history of the company, as well as Walt Disney, the person. They also learn about the company's different divisions and key products, services, and the general future plans for the company.

Most of all, they learn "the Disney Way," which is the approach Walt Disney, and now all cast members, should have toward their roles.

We Are Always on Stage

Cast members learn there are two areas: backstage and on stage. Onstage is any area where you interact with guests. Backstage are those areas behind the scenes where guests are not allowed. While there are some expectations common to both, such as friendliness, honesty, and good grooming habits, the onstage appearance is the one most people probably consider most important.

While onstage, cast members are prohibited from talking about breaks, vacations, sick leave, or anything else associated with a "job" in front of guests. Pulling a cell phone out to check a text message or make a call is cause for discipline. Park guests should feel everyone wants to be there because they *want to be*, and not because they *are paid to be* there.

While it's silly to think guests don't know the person operating the attraction or sweeping the street is paid to be there, they don't need to be reminded of it. Hearing a cast member talk with another cast member about company policies or about what they intend to do after work is inconsistent with the magic of the Magic Kingdom.

The same is true for us. Our guests, customers, and donors will appreciate what we do more when we present it to them as a finished product, rather than inviting them to join us in that production. Especially if we work for a nonprofit, our donors do not want to be reminded that we are paid for our role in the organization.

While no one expects any of us to work for free, that does not mean they want to be told about it. Especially since "overhead" and other expenses are increasingly under scrutiny, we should never talk about our upcoming vacation, raises or promotions, or other issues that remind our donor this is a job.

My first introduction as an adult to a charity was two young employees of a non-profit complaining in front of me about how their recent hotel stay was not up to their standards. The hotel where they stayed is a luxury property, and one (at that time) where I had never stayed. It was too expensive for me. Yet, I was listening to these young people, two decades younger than me, complaining that the resort was not good enough for them. I was about to make a donation to the charity, but had reservations when I realized my donation would not cover even one night at the hotel for these two staffers. It would clearly not be appreciated.

If we work for a for-profit corporation, our customers want to feel they are getting a good deal. If a customer learns about an employee's commission, upcoming sales reward trip to Las Vegas, or other business interests not directly tied to the product or service the customer is purchasing, his immediate thought begins to turn to "I paid too much," and buyer's remorse sets in quickly.

Concentrate on the Guest

As reported in reflectionsonwalt.blogspot.com, in 1994 Judson Green, then the chair of Disney Theme Parks and Resorts, penned a pamphlet for cast members outlining "the daily goal of exceptional performance." His brochure was preparing cast members for the 25th anniversary of the theme park.

He listed the goals to achieve it:

- Exceed guest expectations.
- Get involved.
- Break down barriers.

- Share information and suggestions.
- Work smarter.
- Try new ways to do things.
- Listen to others.
- Be a team player.

He also outlined the importance of Disney heritage and traditions:

- We are committed to a friendly and informal work environment.
- We show our pride and respect for the Disney product and legacy.
- We emphasize cast training and recognition.
- We pursue synergistic opportunities.
- We demonstrate our concern for our environment and community.
- We emphasize "family" entertainment.
- We protect the public's trust in Disney.
- We are committed to education.

None of these are unique to Disney. Anyone who cares for those he serves can use these ideas and ways of doing business to find excellence. In conclusion, Green reminded cast members to "enjoy making guests happy," and to care about fellow cast members as well as their guests.

We Are in the Fantasy Business

While we probably don't have the fantasy setting Disney does, we need to maintain and preserve the fantasy for our donors, guests and customers. When people interact with a nonprofit, they are doing so because they believe in the cause. They are making an emotional investment in its future. This is true no matter what the mission. We need to make the donor feel the organization and the mission is worthy of support, and that the donation or the interaction will be valued and appreciated. Even if the donor comes to us already a hard-core believer, we must do everything we can to assure the donor that their fervent faith is well-placed.

At the same time, with for-profit companies, we want the customer to feel he has spent money wisely on the purchase. I am frequently amazed at all the effort that goes into the sale, then ceases once the sale is completed. For example, when I buy anything electronic, which is often not an inexpensive sum, the first thing the salesperson usually does is try to convince me to purchase the extended warranty.

He just spent some degree of effort to convince me how wonderful the product is and how well it's made, then the pressure comes immediately to convince me that this wonderful product is going to break in the next year or so and why I should spend even more to protect it.

We may not have the fantasy that Disney has, but we all own a piece of it. Donors expect us to be dedicated to the mission. They don't expect us to work for free, but they don't want to be reminded we don't. Customers expect products and services to be fair, reliable, and to perform as advertised.

CHAPTER SEVEN

Believe

Give Them Fireworks

There's a great lesson in Disney's fireworks and it has nothing to do with fire, explosions, or colorful displays. Fireworks, particularly those in the Disney parks, are a lesson in perspective. Undoubtedly, the Disney parks and cruise lines offer spectacular fireworks because they are a magnificent display of creativity, ingenuity, and imagination.

The colorful explosions are carefully choreographed to music, and combined with projected images and flying characters to give an incredible show. No one does it like Disney. Disney wows you with fireworks. They want you to tell others about the beautiful ending to a perfect Disney day. Yet there is another reason why the parks offer fireworks.

Fireworks were not always a part of a visit to Disneyland. They did not start until about a year after opening and were called Fantasy in the Sky. While the fireworks show was created because of the theatrical wonder it offered, there was another more practical reason. In the heat of the day, guests were leaving the park. If they left the park, they were no longer spending money on food, souvenirs, and buying additional tickets to experience more attractions. Disney needed a reason for people to not leave. They needed to give them a reason to stay.

Worth the Stay

With fireworks at the end of the day there was incentive for guests to stay in the park. The allure of a cool pool on a hot day back at the hotel was no longer the best choice. Now, if a guest stayed in the park to see the show at closing, there were more opportunities to sell other things to that guest. The fireworks were free. But the hot dogs, drinks, and t-shirts purchased in the late afternoon were not.

There are two lessons from the fireworks. The first is that no matter what we do, for whatever reason, we will have reasons and motivations for doing it that differ from those of our donors or customers. Even things we think send an obvious message can be seen from an entirely different point of view. The second lesson is that the first lesson is perfectly fine.

Disney offers fireworks because it wants people to stay. Guests see them as a good show. We give and they see for entirely different reasons. Sometimes our points of view are relatively close. Sometimes, far apart. It does not matter.

The lesson we learn from Disney's fireworks is it is perfectly fine for us to do something for one reason and our guests to see it differently. The same is true with Disney's MagicBands. These electronic bracelets, given to park guests, allow them to open their hotel doors, buy tickets and souvenirs, and do just about anything on Disney property simply by waving their wrists over a sensor. Anything that would require money, a key, or a credit card can be accomplished easily when wearing the MagicBand. It replaces them all.

Guests love them and the convenience they offer. Of course, the company appreciates the ease of use it gives guests. However, Disney also likes them for an entirely different reason. It can track the movements and spending habits 24 hours a day of each guest that wears a MagicBand. It gives the company an unprecedented look at consumer behavior and ultimately will allow the company to offer each guest marketing materials and sales pitches that are geared to their individual tastes and habits. It is an incredible micro-marketing niche opportunity. Guests love the bands for one reason. The company loves them for that reason, plus another.

No matter what we do, others will always see our actions and offerings from a different perspective. That is okay. Of course, Disney offers fireworks for their beautiful, spectacular beauty. Guests appreciate them. They would not like them any less if they learned that Disney started them to give guests a reason to stay. In the same way, guests probably realize, but don't necessarily care that their MagicBands give the company an unprecedented insight into their locations and habits. We almost always do things for one reason and our guests see the same action for a different reason. If we ultimately have the comfort, safety, and satisfaction of our guests in mind, rarely does this present a problem.

Saved by a Rainy Day

The magic of the fireworks and even the MagicBands shows the company's almost genetic ability to see things from different points of view. When we approach any problem with that perspective in mind, the outcome can almost always be improved. Walt Disney himself appreciated what could be accomplished when looking at a difficult situation in new ways, even when the problem was a tough one, as this story shows.

Walt was not pleased. He was deep into the production of the studio's first major live-action film, *20,000 Leagues Under the Sea*. The cast and production team were filming the climactic scene where the giant squid attacks the *Nautilus* submarine and its crew. The movie had been leading up to this dramatic showdown where Captain Nemo and his devoted men fight the massive, menacing monster.

However, when the big clash between man and squid was shot, the monster was anything but intimidating. In the DVD commentary with the movie, director Richard Fleisher described the scene as it was shot on set, and the sinking feeling he had as he sat on the soundstage reviewing the footage he had just shot.

He said the scene was a "total disaster" and that "the squid was a terrible looking squid." To make matters worse as he watched the footage, a man came behind him and tapped him on the shoulder. It was Walt Disney. He asked the young director, "What are you filming, a Keystone Comedy?" Disney ordered the scene to be shot again.

Fleisher was in a bind. He had shot the scene exactly as it was written. The script described the battle occurring at sunset with calm seas. The setting meant the wires and cables holding the squid and its tentacles in the air were obvious. The monster's limbs were made of material that absorbed water, so as the shooting progressed, the giant arms drooped, sagged, and lay across the *Nautilus* lifelessly.

The biggest scene in the movie was in serious trouble. The chances for a successful motion picture were as limp as the fake tentacles draped across the fiberglass submarine. Walt Disney told the director to go film another scene not involving the squid. Walt wanted Fleischer to shoot something else so Walt could have time to figure something out.

Walt asked his studio special-effects wizards to construct a better squid, while director Fleischer met with screenwriter Earl Felton. Fleisher credits Felton with saving the scene and the picture. Felton said, "How could we be so stupid?" As Katherine and Richard Greene wrote in their book *The Man Behind the Magic,* Walt's solution was to film at night, and stage the scene during a raging storm. The dark and rain would hide the wires and cables nicely and the storm would add dramatic effect. Now the story also had the added tension of man fighting nature as well as battling the beast.

It was expensive to re-shoot the scene, costing the studio $250,000. Fleischer says it "almost bankrupted the studio." However, the solution to add some rain and turn off the lights not only solved a practical problem, but made the story more compelling and the visual imagery more exciting. It worked.

Even with the greatest and most talented minds in Hollywood working on this major motion picture, the most important scene in the movie was almost a disaster. Bad things happen to good ideas. Sometimes, however, the solution is as simple as changing the background and adding a new element, like rain.

Creativity can often turn the day around. A dilemma of much smaller stature arose for Walt Disney about the same time as the *20,000 Leagues* problems. Walt had wanted a display of the Snow White characters for Disneyland and had ordered European craftsmen to create them. When the statues arrived Walt was stunned to see Snow White was the same height as all the dwarves. She was supposed to be created to scale.

Once discovered, there was not enough time to send them back or re-order. Instead, Disney Imagineers put the statues near the castle in a little grotto. Using a technique called forced perspective, they arranged the statues to give the illusion of proper height. Snow White was placed in the back, while terraced landscaping and a careful choice of foliage around the statues gave the illusion of proper perspective.

Whether we work for a nonprofit or for-profit organization, our success is not always based on how much money we have in our budget. The key is to use what we have carefully. One of the most outstanding qualities of Walt Disney is that he always managed to turn a challenge into an opportunity. So it was with another major project directed by Walt Disney, the Haunted Mansion.

A Chilling Challenge

If you consider Walt Disney's early movies, he recognized the importance of fear in human emotion and decisions. *Snow White*, *Dumbo*, and even some of the Silly Symphonies include a prominent level of fear. Whether it is the isolation of Dumbo or Bambi or the terror of the evil queen in *Snow White*, fear was a constant theme in many of Disney's works.

Before the park even opened, Walt always knew a haunted mansion would be part of Disneyland. The concept is so important that each of Disney's parks around the world today include some form of haunted house attraction.

While the concept of a haunted mansion may have been a priority, it was not a reality for Disneyland on opening day in 1955. Although the park was ready for its haunted mansion, the concept was not ready to be unveiled. It would have to wait. Disneyland's Haunted Mansion is a perfect study on the importance of getting it done right, rather than getting it done quickly.

Even though Disneyland opened in 1955 without a Haunted Mansion, there were sketches and conversations dating back to at least 1951. As Jason Surrell explains in his book *The Haunted Mansion: Imagineering a Disney Classic,* early discussions included various types of mansions (Southern antebellum or New Orleans or Maryland Victorian) and what would be in it. One idea that gained traction for a while was a walk-through exhibit that Walt would call the Museum of the Weird. However, the idea of a Museum of the Weird would be deemed too small to hold all of Walt's and his Imagineer's dreams and ideas.

Room for One More

The Haunted Mansion as we know it today did not open to guests until August 9, 1969. Despite the early sketches and the early notions that Disneyland must include a haunted mansion, the ghosts and spirits had to wait 14 years after the park's opening to materialize. Yet, the Haunted Mansion had a presence in the park much earlier.

A souvenir map depicted the mansion in 1958 and flyers handed out at the main entrance teased the opening in 1963. However, 1963 arrived and departed with no Haunted Mansion. Even though the attraction was not built, the Imagineers had managed to create an outer shell of a Southern plantation home. Marty Sklar, at the start of a career that would lead him to head all Imagineering, drew a sign soliciting "post life-time leases for ghosts and restless spirits," encouraging them to come and join the active retirement of the haunted mansion, club-like atmosphere and scare the daylights out of guests. His sign would be posted outside the façade to encourage ghosts to make the future mansion their home.

The creative sign did attract the excitement and curiosity of Disneyland guests, but did not attract resident spirits until the opening in 1969. The reasons for the delays were several. First, other expansions in Disneyland captured the attention of Walt and his Imagineers, as did the significant presence of Disney at the 1964 World's Fair. But while the Haunted Mansion stewed on the back burner, it grew bigger, more creative, and more astounding than perhaps first imagined. In fact, the shell of the mansion (the exterior) that existed in New Orleans Square since 1963 would not be large enough when completed to house the entire attraction.

As the 1960s were closing, Imagineers worked to complete the mansion. However, if they only completed the shell that had stood in New Orleans Square since 1963, there would not be enough room to hold all their ideas, stories, and special effects. There was plenty of room behind the façade to build the main "show building," but there was one serious problem:

the Disneyland Railroad ran back there. Disney Imagineers had a predicament: how could they build a show building on the other side of the railroad tracks and get guests safely to it?

Stand Down Under

For many other corporations or organizations, the answer would be simple: redesign the attraction to stay on the guest side of the railroad tracks or abandon the idea completely. Others might consider some gate mechanism that would hold back guests while the trains passed. However, with the frequency of the Disneyland trains, and the masses of people expected to visit the Haunted Mansion, gates would not work.

As Imagineers began to tackle the idea of moving guests across the railroad tracks, they quickly came up with a creative solution to the daunting problem. Rather than trying to move guests over the railroad tracks, Disney would take them under.

Today as you enter the Haunted Mansion one of the first rooms you encounter is the Portrait Chamber. Above your head are several paintings of other "guests" as they appeared in their "corruptible, mortal state." They were all drawn by Imagineer Marc Davis.

After you enter the room, the wall seals behind you and you realize the room has no doors and no windows. As the show unfolds, the paintings seemingly begin to stretch. The monologue you hear suggests it is you and the room that are stretching. The portraits reveal the guests that appeared happy and content are now in increasingly perilous positions.

As you stand in the stretching room, you are actually not in a room at all. You are riding a giant elevator. It is taking you and the other guests slowly underground so you can walk safely under the railroad tracks. As the company did with the soggy squid in *20,000 Leagues*, or with the undersized Snow White, they used the problematic hurdles as incentive to jump higher.

When we have a problem that seems insurmountable, we can remember that challenges often offer us the best opportunity to shine. The waterfalls on the Pirates of the Caribbean attraction exist for the same reason. They let the attraction exist beneath other attractions and under the railroad tracks.

The elevator and waterfalls were so effective that the effects were repeated in Florida. However, the Haunted Mansion in Florida does not have an elevator. The ceiling simply rises. And the single waterfall in Florida mirrors the two waterfalls in the Pirates attraction at Disneyland.

Frugal Ghosts

The Haunted Mansion also shows how Disney creates magic on a surprisingly low budget. When creating audio-animatronic figures, the Disney designers took advantage of their work on other projects. In the Grand Hall scene, for example, there are two dueling gentleman who come to life from their portraits and take aim at each other. The duelists are translucent reflections of three-dimensional audio animatronic figures. One of them is taken from the same mold as the auctioneer pirate from the Pirates of the Caribbean.

If you are building a figure for one attraction, rather than create another from scratch, just duplicate the one you already built and dress it in different clothing. That's what the Disney Imagineers did.

Throughout the attraction, many of the figures can be seen in other, less scary settings in other places around the theme park.

With the darkness of the Haunted Mansion and different clothes and facial hair, it's difficult to notice that the dueling gentleman can also be seen auctioning off brides in Pirates of the Caribbean. Many of the presidents in the Hall of Presidents and other audio-animatronic figures do double-duty in the Haunted Mansion and at other attractions as well.

For example, veteran Disneyland guests know the first audio-animatronic figure they approach in the Pirates of the Caribbean is an older man sitting on the dock fishing across from the Blue Bayou Restaurant. He is known as Beacon Joe, and since Pirates opened in 1967 he has sat there plucking his banjo.

The character of Beacon Joe also appears at Walt Disney World. As you round the bend on the riverboat on the Rivers of America, you can see him sitting on a dock, still fishing. He also makes another appearance in Orlando as one of the jailed pirates toward the end of the ride, and he also is in the Haunted Mansion as a ghostly guest in the ballroom scene. He also has made it to Tokyo Disneyland where he appears in its pirate attraction.

When you are making the mold and parts for an audio-animatronic figure, why not make a couple? You can dress them in different outfits with different facial hair or hats and in the stage lighting of the attractions no one knows the difference. Thomas Jefferson, for example, from the Hall of Presidents, is also a sheriff on the Great Move Ride, surrounded by gangsters who are re-purposed pirates.

Disney's World is filled with examples of money-saving ideas that were used to great effect: Disney used the front half of a plane for the Casablanca scene of the Great Movie Ride and the back half of the plane appears in the Jungle Cruise attraction in Disneyland. The steam engine on display at Big Thunder Mountain was used in the movie *Hot Lead, Cold Feet*.

Economy of Scales

In the same way, the large organ at the end of the Haunted Mansion's Grand Hall might look familiar to fans of the movie *20,000 Leagues under the Sea*. The organ is the same one James Mason (Captain Nemo) was playing in the film. It was altered just a little, but why buy or build a new organ when you have one in a warehouse? The organs that appear in subsequent Haunted Mansions are replicas of this one.

Many of the effects in the Haunted Mansion appear sophisticated, but in reality are polished examples of old technology. The transparent ghosts are created using a technique known as Pepper's Ghost. The effect is named for London chemist John Henry Pepper. As told in Jeff Baham's book *The Unauthorized Story of Walt Disney's Haunted Mansion*, Pepper and a colleague, Henry Dirks, published the method for creating the theatrical illusion in 1862. While some guests speculate the appearing and disappearing ghosts are some sort of hologram or laser projection, the reality is the technology of the special effect dates back more than a century before the Haunted Mansion opened.

Shine Surplus Light

Like the replication of audio-animatronic figures, or the use of old movie props, the Disney Company creates many of its magic moments on a surprisingly low budget. Disney purchased the streetlights it would use on Main Street, U.S.A. from the City of Baltimore's used, surplus stock for three cents a pound.

The ornate base of the flagpole in Disneyland's Town Square is the result of a car accident. A car had hit a light pole in Los Angeles on Sunset Boulevard and knocked it over. As reported by Disney Imagineer Rolly Crump in the audio book *More Cute Stories, Disneyland History, Volume 1,* the flag pole base was found by another Disney Imagineer, Emile Kuri, who happened by the scene where work crews were removing the damaged pole. The ornately decorated base was solid metal and would be a beautiful addition to Disneyland. Kuri purchased the 60- to 80-pound base for 35 cents a pound. It became the base of the flag pole that now stands in the center of Town Square.

With little money for landscaping, Walt asked Bill Evans to collect "specimen trees" to help bring his prized Jungle Cruise to life. Evans scoured neighborhoods offering to buy up trees in homeowners' yards. In some cases, he would plant trees upside down, with the roots in the air. He would then grow vines on the roots to create exotic looking foliage.

In Crump's book *It's Kind of a Cute Story*, he recalls how he sculpted the animatronics for the Enchanted Tiki Room. "I sculpted the tikis right there in the parking lot. You might think that the people sculpting for Disney have got these gorgeous temperature-controlled rooms filled with North light to better aid their work. But no.... You know what I sculpted with? A plastic fork...right out of the studio's cafeteria." While it is easy to think we need a huge budget to do great things, Disney proved much can be done with little. It's not the budget that limits accomplishment. We are limited only by our imagination.

Off the Shelf

Disney was recycling and repurposing long before it was popular. What ideas do we have that can be repurposed or re-used in a slightly different way? If something works, use it and continue using it. Don't re-invent the wheel. In the same way, Disney never has failures. It just has ideas that are not quite right, or whose time has not yet come.

Walt Disney would say, "Get a good idea and stay with it. Dog it and work at it until it's done, and done right." The Disney company, like its namesake, never gives up on an idea. It keeps drawers and file cabinets of ideas, shows, and attractions that were never built. Sometimes they are revived, sometimes forgotten, sometimes parts of some are combined to create a new attraction.

If you have invested in something that is not quite right, don't throw it away. Store it for another day. Never waste an idea. Walt had asked Imagineer John Hench to design a trip through space as a new centerpiece attraction for the remodeled Tomorrowland. The ride was eventually shelved for Anaheim, but built as Space Mountain in Florida. It was also later built in California.

Don't let failures have the final word. The lovable Country Bear Jamboree attraction was created by

Disney designer Marc Davis for a ski resort Disney had planned called Mineral King, near Yosemite National Park. Walt figured skiers would come from the slopes and want to be entertained. The Mineral King project never matured, but the attraction envisioned for it was there for the opening of Walt Disney World.

The High Cost of Printing

In the 1950s, it cost Disney 24 cents to print the *Disneyland Souvenir Guide*. As reported by Rich Hamilton in *Disney Magic Ideabook*, the company sold each guide book for 25 cents which meant it was losing money or breaking even with every sale. The merchandising department urged Walt Disney to increase the price of the guide so they could make a profit. Walt said, "I don't care about making money on this. ... I want as many of these guide books as possible on people's coffee tables. I want others to see what Disneyland is about and come for a visit. We'll make money when they actually come to Disneyland." Incidentally, one of the first salesmen of these guidebooks was a young man who we now know as comedian Steve Martin.

Floral Dresses

Cypress Gardens, which Walt studied before opening Disneyland, was an early attraction in central Florida, not far from where Walt Disney World would eventually be built. Cypress Gardens was Florida's first theme park and featured lush, landscaped gardens and a water ski show on Winter Haven's Lake Eloise. Walt knew the park's owner and founder, Dick Pope, and visited him as he worked on the Disneyland project.

A major feature of Cypress Gardens was young lady employees that guests would encounter as they wandered through the gardens. Known as Southern Belles, they were featured on countless postcards and in endless rolls of tourist film. However, the idea for the Southern Belles did not come from a marketing study. Rather, Pope and his wife, Julie, created the idea of the Southern Belle in response to a crisis.

The story goes that in the early 1940s a frost had killed much of the flowers and bushes at the entrance to Cypress Gardens. The Popes realized that if people saw the dead plants out front, they would not want to come in and would not buy tickets. To keep them from turning away, Julie Pope dressed some female employees in Civil War-era hoopskirts and lined them up in front of the dead plants to hide the foliage. From that moment until the closing of Cypress Gardens in 2003, the Cypress Gardens Southern Belles were some of the most photographed women in the world, and they walked the park year-round.

They key to all the challenges that face us is to see them for what they are: opportunities. Disney had to move guests over railroad tracks when he realized a better alternative would be to take them under the tracks. The solution to get people into a horticultural park when some of the plants along the entrance had died is to add color in other areas so people do not notice or care about the dead plants. Some of the greatest innovations at Walt Disney World arose from a need to solve a problem. While our problems are as unique as we are, we can all remember that sometimes the greatest opportunities arrive at our doorstep in a package labeled, "Big Problem."

What Is Our Business?

To find creative solutions to big problems, look at your business to determine if you are in the business you think you are. If we asked someone at a restaurant what he or she did, the response might be, "I serve food." While it is certainly true the restaurant serves food, what it does is something different. Its business is not to serve food. It is to give people a treat, and to give them an *experience* that is more attractive than eating at home.

A financially disappointing example of not knowing what business one is in can be found in our nation's historic railroads. Railroads were crucial in the expansion of the United States, and also played an important role in the design of Disneyland. Yet, despite the power and importance held almost exclusively by the railroads, they never stopped to ask, "What business are we in?"

From the mid-1850s and for the next hundred years, rail travel was the dominant way of moving people and freight across the United States. Railroad travel was so important, it gave us many of the great "robber barons" and other philanthropists whose profits continue to fund charities today: Vanderbilt, Carnegie, Stanford, Morgan, and others. Many cities today owe their names (for better or worse) to the railroad officials whose trains were heading west.

As railroads progressed across the western frontier, it was often the railroad companies that built whole towns and gave them their names. Conductors could then call out names in alphabetical order, making it easier for the conductor to remember and say the names, and easier for passengers to listen for and know how much longer they would need to ride. For example, if you live in the Nebraska towns of Crete, Exeter, Fairfield, Glenville or Harvard, your town was named by a railroad official more than a century ago. Railroads not only opened the West, but named it as well.

Today, however, if you asked someone to name a railroad, they would probably mention Amtrak. Perhaps you might hear CSX, Union Pacific, Santa Fe, or Norfolk and Southern. Gone are the dozens of passenger train rail lines that once crossed our nation. As late as the 1950s, railroads were still the most popular and most efficient way of getting between cities. Walt Disney loved railroads and if you ride the Disneyland railroad today, you might notice each of the five locomotives have names.

Walt named locomotive number one, the *C.K. Holliday*, after Cyrus Kurtz Holliday, the founder of the Santa Fe Railroad. Walt named locomotive number two, the *E.P. Ripley*, after Edward Payson Ripley, an early president of the Atchison, Topeka and Santa Fe Railroad. Fred Gurley was the chair of the Atchison, Topeka and Santa Fe Railroad when Disneyland opened, and he too was honored by Walt Disney with his name on a Disney locomotive. The *Ernest S. Marsh* honors the man who headed the Santa Fe Railroad when Disneyland opened its doors, and the *Ward Kimball*, the newest addition to the Disneyland stock, honors Disney animator and train enthusiast, Ward Kimball.

If asked, any of the men honored with their names on any of Disneyland's locomotives or any of their peers from now-defunct railroads would have likely said they were in the "railroad business." Unwittingly, they mistook what they did for who they were. They were not in the railroad business. They were in the transportation business.

The railroad owners and operators had perhaps the largest monopoly of any corporation in their time. They could alter the fortunes of communities and even state economies with decisions about where rails would be placed. To move anything anywhere you had to hire the railroad. So naturally, anyone in that business would say they are in the rail business.

Had they answered that they were in the transportation business, our world would look much different today. Perhaps we would ride on airplanes owned by railroads. Maybe we would board a 747 on New Haven Airlines. The railroads saw the coming of the automobile and airplane, but never saw them as competitors. Had they seen the threat, they would have adopted and branched out into other areas.

They had mastered railroading and went to bed each night comfortable that no one could *railroad* like they could *railroad*. Yet, the people who owned and ran the railroads never minded their business, or at least as much as they could have. They were in the transportation business and the transportation business was leaving railroads behind. While today's railroad companies move massive amounts of freight efficiently and profitably, the airlines have taken away almost all passenger traffic and a portion of the freight business.

It's in the Soup

Begin each day be reminding yourself what your business is. The difference is between what you do and how you do it. If you are a food bank, how you do your business is to gather and distribute food. What you do is give people hope. You help families survive. On the for-profit side, think about theaters. What they do is show movies. How they do it is by selling an entertainment experience. The popcorn, lobby, and even the communal nature of watching a movie with others are all key ingredients. Movie theaters would not exist, if all they did was show movies. Many theater owners consider themselves to be in the concession business and not the movie business. It's no wonder. Statistics show popcorn has a 900% mark-up. Without popcorn, movie theaters would be out of business.

Never confuse what we do for how we do it. Donors and customers want to know what you do. They already have a pretty good idea of how you do it. If we run a Hawaiian music school, we shouldn't tell parents and students we will teach them all how to play the ukulele. That's how we do it. What we are doing is teaching them discipline and a new form of self-expression while giving them self-confidence as they learn to play the ukulele.

What we do is always more important than how we do it. Even if ukuleles disappear, we could still accomplish the same result with banjos, guitars, or harmonicas. Sell what you do. Donors (and customers) will buy that. Donors, guests, and customers can be passionate about what you do. How you do it doesn't always matter as much.

Disney does not create cartoons. It brings animated features to life.

What we do is the stuff of dreams and aspirations. How we do it is the steps and procedures we teach to new hires. While "how we do" is literally what we do all day, it is mechanical, repeatable, mundane. "What we do" is the reason why we do the "how."

The World's Largest Hotel Chain

It is easy to confuse "how" and "what." Consider a major hotel chain that will remain nameless. For years, all of its print and television advertisements contained the tagline, "The world's largest hotel chain." If you were to ask someone in the chain why they were successful, they might say it is because they have more hotels than anyone else. Having the most rooms is how they make money. It is not what they did to get there.

The chain became the largest because, perhaps, of its attention to cleanliness, or because of its convenient locations. It could be for any number of reasons. What they did was pay attention to the customer somehow, some way. Too bad they did not tap into that when they came up with their slogan.

For years the slogan worked. Board members could read reports and high-five each other because each spreadsheet would confirm they were the largest in the world. Just as the Evil Queen in *Snow White* would ask the mirror who was the fairest in the land, the hotel company would ask, "Who is the largest in the land," and it would always get the same answer, "You are." For years the answers came like clockwork and the board could rejoice in its chain being the largest. But, "biggest" does not last forever.

Through growth or mergers, or other means, another hotel group suddenly had more hotels than they did. No longer could they boast they were the largest. That honor belonged to another. And as the crown passed, so did the slogan. The new "largest" chain would soon boast "more hotels than anyone in the world."

Perhaps these slogans about size were the result of massive consumer testing and focus groups. Maybe the travelers of the world were clamoring to stay in a record-setting hotel chain. However, this is not likely. How many people, when reserving a room, or when bleary-eyed on the interstate and are looking for a place to stay would choose a place because it was part of the largest hotel chain? People search for something more meaningful to them.

Who Are We Trying to Please?

While having the most of anything sounds great to a board and shareholders, it does not usually sound good to customers, or to donors in the non-profit world. Maybe the major hotels chains were just a little off in their messaging. Maybe what they were really trying to say was that, "No matter where you go, you'll have friend there waiting for you with a familiar, clean, comfortable room," or words to that effect.

Maybe the new slogan, which might show what being the biggest means to the customer, could be: "Hotels everywhere, for every need." Or on the same website, an even more refined version of the same sentiment, "We're everywhere you need to go," or even more simply, "We're there for you." If you like the hotel here, you will like it there, because your friend in the hotel in Peoria is just like the friend you will meet behind the desk in Omaha. You turn the size advantage from bottom-line braggadocio to a front-line attempt to lure and please more customers. Give them what they want. A board may care about being the biggest. The guest just wants to get a good night's sleep—and can only stay in one hotel at a time.

Job Descriptions

Everything in every Disney park is designed around the simple premise: every guest is a V.I.P. When your "what" is "every guest is a V.I.P.," then your "how" takes care of itself. When every guest is special, you design your storefront windows on Main Street, U.S.A. closer to the ground so children can easily see inside. With a deliberate attempt to make every guest feel royally welcome, you paint the sidewalks on Main Street red to subtly remind them they are stars walking on the red carpet to be part of the show.

If you were to talk to the architect working on Main Street's construction, and asked what his job was, he would say, "My job is to design the windows so youngsters can see inside easily." He would not say, "My job is to design windows low to the ground." While the difference is a couple of letters on paper, it represents oceans of difference in attitude in getting things done. One looks at things from a "job" point of view. The other looks at things from what you hope to accomplish with your job. If you can master this, you are well on your way to customer, donor, and guest relations the Disney way.

CHAPTER EIGHT

A Great Big Beautiful Tomorrow

As we go about our jobs and lives, we too should look for ways to innovate and create new possibilities. The most dangerous statement anyone or any organization could ever make is, "That's the way we've always done it." As we strive to make our organizations and ourselves better, the only way to do it is to do it like no one else has ever done before.

Although Walt Disney created an entertainment empire, he never seemed to take it for granted. As he was fond of saying, "It all started with a mouse." For us, it begins and ends with our mission. As we strive do be more like Disney, we must always find new and innovative ways to serve and impress our guests, but we should also remember where we came from, that it all began from something much humbler. Walt was always in touch with his tough Kansas childhood.

In the film *Saving Mr. Banks*, Walt Disney, portrayed by Tom Hanks, explained to *Mary Poppins* author P.L. Travers how his childhood influenced his life as an adult. Memories of his youth were never far away. He described how he and his big brother Roy delivered newspapers, both the morning and evening editions, for their father, Elias Disney, in Kansas City:

> Winters were harsh. ... Old Elias didn't believe in new shoes until the old ones were wore through. ... Rare is the day I don't think of that eight-year-old boy [speaking of himself] delivering papers in the snow.

Walt's childhood influenced almost every decision he made. From those modest beginnings, Walt always kept the guest in mind. "Disney guests *must* feel that they received their money's worth in entertainment. Our audience is not a 'one time shot,' but the key to our future success. We want them coming back and we want them telling their friends that 'it was worth every cent.'"

Roy

When Walt delivered those newspapers for his father, he knew he would never be alone. He could always count on his big brother, Roy. Walt and Roy shared a challenging childhood and would not only grow up together, but work together all their lives. They were never far from one another.

We all need someone we can rely on; someone who will always be there for us. We need someone we can share ideas with, and someone who knows he or she can tell us when we are right, when we are wrong, or when we need to hold back. For Walt, that person was Roy. We all need a Roy. Who is your Roy?

Walt was the idea man; the creative force. Roy was the money man; the banker. Roy would hear Walt's ideas and figure out a way to pay for them. As Walt said, Roy restrained him. Roy was the stabilizing force to Walt's wild swings of imagination. Rather than being hampered by Roy, Walt understood the need for Roy, and Roy recognized his brother had the artistry and drive he would never have.

Roy's fondness for Walt would continue after his brother's death. Originally, the Florida Project was to be called Disney World. After Walt's death, Roy insisted the name be changed to Walt Disney World, so everyone would always know whose idea it was. Walt would never see the completion of Walt Disney World, but Roy would guide the project to its successful opening. After dedicating the park in October 1971, Roy would join his brother in death just two months later.

Take the Stairs Two at a Time

One of the most remarkable accomplishments of the Disney brothers is who they hired. As they built the Disney organization, they had a knack for finding people who shared not only a tremendous talent, but an enthusiasm for the work set forth by Walt and Roy.

In the mid 1990s I wanted to write a book about Disney cast members and what it was like to work at the happiest place on earth. I interviewed friends who worked for Disney who then introduced me to new friends. The discussions I had with cast members gave me fantastic insight into the Disney organization and showed me the depth of love so many cast members had for their company, their friends, and for the guests they entertain each day.

One such cast member was Bub Thomas.

If you know Bub, you know Disney.

If you had been to Walt Disney World in 1997 or before, you probably saw Charles David Thomas. Known as "Bub" to friends and generations of Disney visitors, Bub was a member of the Dapper Dans Barbershop Quartet. The group sings to guests each day on Main Street, U.S.A. Even at age 85, Bub would sing, dance, and tell jokes to thousands of people each day, along with the other three talented members in their brightly colored pinstripe suits.

Bub started with the barbershop quartet in Disneyland, but moved to Florida in 1971 to help open the new park. Even before the first guests arrived, Bub and his friends would sing for the construction workers and employees to help make them laugh and feel good as opening day loomed closer.

Sketchy Work

What the thousands of guests would never know about Bub is that his fame spread around the world—not only for his singing, but for his artwork. Years ago, a young fan with a life-threatening illness had asked Bub for a drawing and Bub drew a quick sketch of the child on a large, white Disney envelope and mailed it to her.

Doctors saw the drawing and asked Bub to do another for a second, young patient. It did not stop there. As more requests came in, Bub would ask for a photo of the child and what activity the child liked to do. If the child's interest was water skiing, Bub would draw a fun caricature of the child on skis.

When Bub was not singing on Main Street, he would rush up to his office to answer the many requests that came to him daily. He would draw a dozen or more such greetings each day and send them around the world. Bub loved doing this. He was not paid to make the drawings. He created them during his break times. Even after retiring from the Dapper Dans, Disney continued paying Bub as a Disney ambassador and he continued coming to Walt Disney World to continue drawing for children who asked.

The Wonderful Thing about Bub

I was fortunate to interview Bub and had the privilege of following him to his small office just above Main Street. There he had letters pinned to his wall where doctors and children had written thank-you notes and words of encouragement. Next to his still uncashed check pinned to the wall from Walt Disney World in the 1970s, correspondence and photographs from the Golden Age of Hollywood lined his walls. Bub had performed with Mel Torme, Gene Autry, and Bob Hope. He had traveled to Vietnam and entertained the troops on the front lines. He told me, "I would go into the back areas and entertain the troops where the big names would not go." Bub said his job was to "entertain people and make them happy."

He did.

Months after I interviewed him, and just weeks after his yellow Dapper Dans costume was retired from Walt Disney World in a colorful ceremony, Bub was killed in a car accident. Knowing that Bub and I had talked in depth, the Disney company asked me to write his obituary. I wrote it and it appeared on the front page of *Eyes and Ears*, the cast member newspaper, the week of his death.

I stretched for words to describe someone who had affected so many for so long. How do you illustrate a life like his? Here is an excerpt of what I offered to *Eyes and Ears* (and what eventually was published) in my attempt to capture some of his life and show the influence he had while giving Disney cast members something fitting to remember him:

Charles "Bub" Thomas

The man behind 25 years of music on Main Street has died. On Tuesday, January 28, 1997, Charles "Bub" Thomas was driving to work at the Magic Kingdom when he was killed in a car accident. Bub created Walt Disney World's Dapper Dans, a barbershop quartet that performs daily on Main Street.

Recently, he celebrated his 85th birthday. While most people retire long before 85, he never tired. His schedule and energy would frustrate a teenager. As recently as last fall he could be seen on Main Street singing and dancing with the Dapper Dans.

Bub worked at Walt Disney World before there was a Walt Disney World. Two weeks before the official park opening, construction workers from the Disney property were invited into the Magic Kingdom for a test run. He thought it was ironic that the construction workers who had worked so hard for years on the Disney project would leave just as it was opening. He wanted to do something special for the workers. Since then, he has performed with Meredith Wilson and he portrayed Uncle Sam in Walt Disney World's America on Parade bicentennial celebration.

For Bub, the sweetest music was not the notes, but the space between them. Besides being a respected singer, he was also a gifted artist, a skill he learned during his burlesque and nightclub days. When he was not singing with the Dapper Dans, he would bound up the steps to his second-story office two at a time. There he received cards and letters from doctors all over the country. They would send Bub pictures of sick and terminally ill children, along with descriptions of the children's interests. He would then draw a caricature of the child playing baseball, water skiing, or anything the child wanted. Walt Disney World provided oversized, 10x14 white envelopes to Bub. He then drew the caricatures on these envelopes and sent them back to the children. Bub responded to every letter the same day he received them. On a recent day, he mailed 14 letters to children. When he stopped singing last fall, he devoted all his time to helping children.

Bub and the music he made may be gone, but his office is not silent. The walls there sing loudly of his tireless efforts to brighten the lives of others. Dozens of pictures line the walls. Celebrities, family, children, and friends all smile down on the chair where Bub used to draw his pictures. Against one wall, there are three file cabinets. Each has four drawers. Each drawer overflows with letters from children and doctors thanking him. He has donated his time and money to other charities as well. Today, a California Lion's Club eye center building bears Bub Thomas' name.

In 1969, he performed with the USO in Vietnam. As he returned from the tour he wrote in his diary, "Sunday, November 24, 1969—OH HAPPY DAY!!! I hope Joyce is as glad to see me as I was to see her and the kids. Great Trip."

Great Trip, Bub.

Although I am pleased with the words I wrote, the one thing that describes Bub best is not words, but am image. It is one I referenced in the obituary, and one that was picked up by the *Orlando Sentinel* in its obituary which was written after mine. Even at age 85, Bub would take the steps two at a time. He could not wait to get to his office and respond to children's letters. His excitement of getting "to work" carried him up the stairs with a speed and enthusiasm not reflecting his body's age. His magic stood out in a land known for magic and wonder.

At his funeral, dozens of the finest Disney entertainers paid their respects. There was a eulogy from the leader of Disney's band. There was singing, dancing, and laughing amid the crying. Like so many Disney movies, this was a Disney funeral, and it had it all. The funeral home in Orlando has never seen a funeral like it before and will never see one like it again.

When our story is told, remember that many of the things we do won't matter much after we are gone. What people will remember, and what will continue to affect others for generations, is our approach, our attitude, and our outlook. My prayer for my life and for all those who read these pages is that no matter what we do in life, or what we do for a living, may it always be said that we took the steps two at a time.

Stop Talking, Start Doing

Walt Disney had a saying that more than any other described his outlook on life and on his work: "The way to get started is to stop talking and start doing." As our journey through this book comes to a close, I hope you have found inspiration to try things you have not tried before. Perhaps you have been prompted to start that project you have always been thinking about. Maybe you have made a call you have been reluctant to make. Even with clear victories and major successes behind him, scores of people were willing to throw water on the fire of Disney's imagination. Don't let naysayers naysay you. They will always be with you.

Thinking about your best is never as good as trying your best. Make your movie. Tape your television show. Build your Disneyland. Rest assured, though, that Disneyland was not built in a day. It was built over long years, one piece at a time, and as Walt said, "Disneyland will never be completed. It will continue to grow as long as there is imagination left in the world." We don't have to complete that amazing project—only start it.

Many victories are scored simply by turning intention into action. It's alright to continue working on a project. That is one of the primary reasons why Walt Disney built Disneyland. "A picture is a thing that once you wrap it up and turn it over to Technicolor, you're through. ... The last picture I just finished...it's gone. I can't touch it. I wanted something I could keep 'plussing' with ideas. The park is that." If you have an idea, talk about it enough to get started, then do just that.

As long as we are honest, authentic, and are looking out for our customer and our company (or organization), we can try anything. The secret is to "do," not "say." Walt also said, "There's really no secret about our approach. We keep moving forward, opening up new doors and doing new things because we're curious... and curiosity keeps leading us down new paths."

The Plans You Dream

I close this book with two of my favorite stories about Walt Disney. As he spent his final hours in the hospital, he could look out the window and see his studio, which was just across the street. Walt was never far from his happiest place on earth.

Walt's big brother Roy was there as Walt lay dying. The brothers who started together from such humble

> "Give the people everything you can give them, keep it clean, friendly, and make it a real fun place to be, and I think that will hang on after Disney."
>
> —Walt Disney

beginnings so many decades before had been together all their lives and were together now. They had worked together in Kansas City and moved together to California. Walt dreamed. Roy paid the bills.

Now the older brother was rubbing the feet of his younger brother, watching the life that was so much larger than life slip from Walt's ever-youthful eyes. As the legend goes, as Walt lay in the hospital bed, he asked Roy to look at the ceiling above the bed with him.

Using the square acoustic ceiling tiles as a grid, he showed his brother where the main buildings for EPCOT would be. Walt pointed and motioned as if the entire property were mapped out on the overhead grid. "Over there is the monorail station. There is the main business tower," Walt would continue as he pulled his brother closer to his side to see EPCOT with him.

In his mind, as he'd done with Disneyland years before, Walt could visualize EPCOT and his "Florida Project" as clearly as if he were looking at a photograph. Even when he had no future, he never stopped planning the future and its promised possibilities.

As Walt's death spread through the studio and the world, cast members at the studio left his office undisturbed. It was as if everyone expected this all to be a bad dream. Surely, this dark period would end and have a Disney-style finale when the prince, Walt, would come back through the doors, and everything would return to normal. How could there be a Disney without Walt?

On Walt's untouched desk is the source of my second favorite Disney legend. On his desk was a handwritten note that merely read, "Kurt Russell." No one knows what it meant, or why it was there. But just as he had envisioned EPCOT, he was probably thinking of the young star for a role in a new movie. No one will ever know.

In his will Walt Disney left a large portion of his estate to the California Institute of the Arts (Cal Arts), an institution he helped found. He also gave to the Jules Stein Eye Institute, the Children's Hospital of Orange County, and the Los Angeles Zoo.

Yet, while his monetary gifts had a prominent, immediate impact for those non-profits and the people they serve, Walt gave us something else, perhaps even more profound. Walt taught us all how to look at the world in a new way. He showed how a poor farm boy and his brother from the Midwest could build a media empire based on sheer will and determination.

As we set out to sell our products, film our movies, or build the non-profit causes that are the foundation of our lives, may we always follow Walt's lead. Above all, may we change the world for the better in our own ways, just as he did. As Walt showed, the real impact is not what we do for ourselves, but how we do everything for others.

Afterword

Everyone is familiar with Walt Disney, whether through animation, film, television, or Disneyland. Dig deeper and you'll find these ventures were built on unique, proven principles—ones that apply to any organization. Many folks assume that any activity specializes in their niche activity. Not true. All are in the *people business* first. Specialty success comes after people success.

What better mentor than Walt Disney, especially with the fantastically successful Disneyland. Walt Disney asked me to join him in creating Disneyland, as one of his original eighteen Imagineers in 1954. As one of only two surviving members, I was there from the start. I learned first hand why Walt was so successful. What Wayne has learned first hand are Walt's guiding principles—and he now shares those vast lessons learned in his new book, *The Disney Difference*.

While these lessons were developed in a themed entertainment enterprise, Disneyland, they apply to all organizations. *The Disney Difference* is jam-packed with exquisite details of Walt's principles and why they work everyday in the real world. They focus on *the people*.

If you're contemplating a new people enterprise, or want to improve an existing business, you cannot find a better reference manual for success than *The Disney Difference*.

— Bob Gurr, Disney Imagineer

Selected Bibliography

In addition to interviews, conversations, and observations, the following books, websites, and articles were sources of information and inspiration for this book.

"The Matterhorn Bobsleds at Disneyland: Innovations in Steel." EntertainmentDesigner.com, June 11, 2011.

Ackert, David G. *40 Years in a Mousetrap*. Theme Park Press, 2015.

Baby, Soman. "Drive Through Post Office." *Gulf Digital News*, July 19, 2007.

Baham, Jeff. DoomBuggies.com/secrets_ballroom.php.

Baham, Jeff. *The Unauthorized Story of Walt Disney's Haunted Mansion*. Theme Park Press, 2014.

Beckwith, Harry. *Selling the Invisible*. Warner Books, 1997.

Blanchard, Ken, with Kathy Cuff and Vicki Halsey. *Legendary Service*. McGraw Hill, 2014.

Broggie, Michael. *Walt Disney's Railroad Story*. Pentrex, 1997.

Burr, Chandler. "Hotels' New Custom Scents." *Travel and Leisure*, April 14, 2009.

Busch Entertainment Corporation. *Busch Gardens, The Dark Continent Employment Booklet*, 1987.

Busch Entertainment Corp. *The Dark Continent, Busch Gardens, Operations Department Manual*, circa 1980.

Cockerell, Lee. *Creating Magic*. Crown Business, 2008.

Crump, Rolly and Jeff Heimbuch. *It's Kind of a Cute Story*. Bamboo Forest Publishing, 2011.

DeGaetano, Steve. *The Disneyland Railroad*. Theme Park Press, 2015.

DeGaetano, Steve. *The Ward Kimball*. Theme Park Press, 2015.

Dunn, Julie. "The Duck Quacks and Has a Big Bill." *New York Times*, November 12, 2000.

Finnie, Shaun. *The Disneylands that Never Were*. LuLu, 2006.

Gaschler, Dean. *I Led the Parade!* Legacy Book Publishing, 2013.

Gennawey, Sam. *The Disneyland Story*. Keen Communications, 2014.

Greene, Katherine and Richard Greene. *The Man Behind the Magic*. Penguin Group, 1991.

Hamilton, Rich. *Disney Magic Ideabook*. Sellbetter Tools, 2004.

Hench, John and Peggy Van Pelt. *Designing Disney*. Disney Editions, 2003.

Johnson, John. "Coonskin Cap Clings to Crockett." *Los Angeles Times*, August 23, 2002.

Joyce, Alan. *Secrets of the Mouse*. Alan Joyce, 2008.

Koenig, David. *Mouse Tales*. Bonaventure Press, 1994.

Koenig, David. *Mouse Tales, Golden Anniversary Special Edition*. Bonaventure Press, 2005.

Koenig, David. *Realityland*. Bonaventure Press, 2007.

Korkis, Jim. *Secret Stories of Walt Disney World*. Theme Park Press, 2015.

Linder Fitzpatrick, Lillian. "Nebraska Place Names." University of Nebraska Studies in Language, Literature, and Criticism, 1925.

Lipp, Doug. *Disney U*. McGraw Hill Education, 2013.

Martín, Hugo. "Thrill Ride Designers Compete to Push the Limits." *Los Angeles Times,* March 13, 2012.

McKenzie, Richard B. *Why Popcorn Costs So Much at the Movies*. Springer, 2008.

Miller, Michael. "'Bumping the Lamp,' Disney Style." *Denver Business Journal*, March 19, 2000.

Money.cnn.com/galleries/2010/news/1001/gallery.americas_biggest_ripoffs/2.html.

Nass, Herbert E., Esq. *Wills of the Rich and Famous*. Warner Books, 1991.

Paik Sunoo, Brenda. "How Fun Flies at Southwest Airlines." WorkForce.com, June 1, 1995.

Pierce, Todd James. *Three Years in Wonderland*. The University of Mississippi Press/Jackson 2016.

Pope, Dick. *Water Skiing*. Prentice-Hall, 1958.

Price, Harrison "Buzz". *Walt's Revolution! By the Numbers*. Ripley Entertainment, 2003.

Sanborn, Mark. *The Fred Factor: How Passion in your Work and Life Can Turn the Ordinary into the Extraordinary*. Currency Doubleday, 2004.

Shenot, Christine. "Friends Remember Main Street Legend." *Orlando Sentinel*, January 30, 1997.

Sklar, Marty. *One Little Spark!* Disney Editions, 2015.

Smith, Dave. *Disney Facts Revealed*. Disney Editions, 2016.

Smith, Dave. *Disney Trivia from the Vault*. Disney Enterprises, 2012.

Snow, Dennis. *Lessons from the Mouse*. DC Press, 2009.

Surrell, Jason. *Pirates of the Caribbean*. Disney Editions, 2005.

Surrell, Jason. *The Haunted Mansion: Imagineering a Disney Classic*. Disney Editions, 2d ed., 2015.

The Disney Institute. *Be Our Guest*. Disney Editions, 2001.

The Imagineers. *Walt Disney Imagineering*. Hyperion, 1996.

The Walt Disney Company. *The Magic Is You! A Guide to Your Role in the Show*. 1990.

The Walt Disney Company. *Welcome to Walt Disney World, A Cast Member's Handbook*. Circa 1985.

The Walt Disney Company. *Your Role in the Walt Disney World Show*. 1987.

Thornton, David. "From Swampland Came Tourists' Eden." *The Tampa Tribune*, October 30, 1994.

Veness, Susan. *The Hidden Magic of Walt Disney World*. Adams Media, 2009.

Walt Disney Productions. *20,000 Leagues Under the Sea Special Edition DVD*, Commentary.

WDWMagic.com/threads/disney-world-hotel-rooms. 74271.

WDWMagic.com/walt-disney-world-history.htm (quoting a 2009 Walt Disney Company press release).

Yesterland.com/disneylandsign.html.

Zorn, Eric. "Time Stands Still When You Are Waiting in Line at the Post Ofofice." *Chicago Tribune*, March 5, 2007.

About the Author

Wayne Olson grew up in the shadow of Walt Disney World. A frequent visitor to the Magic Kingdom since 1971, Wayne stopped counting trips to the Magic Kingdom at 1,000. At the age of 16, Wayne began work in the operations department at Busch Gardens Tampa, where over the course of several seasons he was trained and operated almost every ride in the park, including the monorail, steam train, and jungle cruise.

Today, Wayne speaks on customer and donor relations all over the country. He is a frequent presenter at international conferences and has clients from Alaska to Florida. Numerous organizations and corporations call on him as a keynote speaker and trainer each year. He also writes for a national publisher where his work is used by hundreds of charities in their websites, newsletters, and brochures. In 2014, *Fundraising Success Magazine* named him "Most Inspiring Speaker."

Wayne teaches nonprofit and for-profit corporations how to relate better to their donors, customers, and employees. He also trains boards on governance and sales, and teaches a course on sales and on nonprofit fundraising at the University of Alabama in Huntsville School of Professional and Continuing Studies. In addition to this book, Wayne is the author of *Think Like a Donor* and *Big Gifts, Small Effort*.

Wayne also hosts a radio show, and regularly appears on podcasts and broadcasts presented by other organizations and experts. He is a former television producer and trial lawyer. Often, his advice includes counseling clients to be just a little more like Walt Disney. To invite Wayne to speak to your company, group, or organization, contact him at wayneolson.com or wayne@wayneolson.com. Wayne can be followed on twitter at @waynero.

More Books from Theme Park Press

Theme Park Press is the largest independent publisher of Disney, Disney-related, and general interest theme park books in the world, with dozens of new releases each year.

Our authors include Disney historians like Jim Korkis and Didier Ghez, Disney animators and artists like Mel Shaw and Eric Larson, and such Disney notables as Van France, Tom Nabbe, and Bill "Sully" Sullivan, as well as many promising first-time authors.

We're always looking for new talent.

In March 2016, we published our 100th title. For a complete catalog, including book descriptions and excerpts, please visit:

ThemeParkPress.com

Learn the Secrets of Walt Disney's Success

Acclaimed Disney expert Jim Korkis tells the stories of what Walt did right, what he did wrong, and how you can follow in his footsteps. Packed with lessons, anecdotes, and quotes, this practical book is all you need to master the Disney way.

From Marceline to the Magic Kingdom

Award-winning Associated Press reporter Bob Thomas' original biography of Walt Disney is fast-moving and insightful—the perfect introduction to Walt for readers of all ages.

Did Walt Really Say That?

Now you'll know for sure, in this comprehensive collection of Walt Disney's wisdom, as delivered through interviews, articles, speeches, TV appearances, and more. Each of the over 800 quotes in this book is sourced as well. You'll be surprised by what Walt said—and what he didn't say!

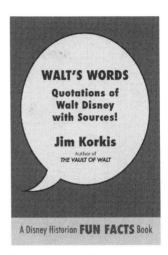

themeparkpress.com/books/walts-words.htm

Walt Disney and the Pursuit of Progress

Walt Disney is synonymous with animation, theme parks, and Mickey Mouse. But his real passion was technology. Documentary filmmaker Christian Moran, along with Rolly Crump, Bob Gurr, and a trio of prominent Disney historians, explore Walt's fascination with technology.

themeparkpress.com/books/great-big-beautiful-tomorrow.htm

Put Walt to Work for You

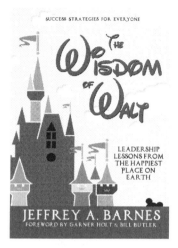

How do you go from dreaming of a theme park to building one? Walt Disney laid the blueprint. Learn how he did it, and how his wisdom can guide you toward achieving the things that you dream of.

themeparkpress.com/books/wisdom-walt.htm

Learn from the Disney Imagineers

Creativity. Innovation. Success. That's Disney Imagineering. It was the Imagineers who brought Walt Disney's dreams to life. Now *you* can tap into the principles of Imag-ineering to make *your* personal and profession-al dreams come true.

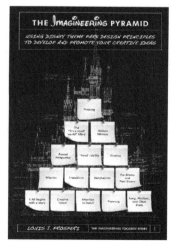

themeparkpress.com/books/imagineering-pyramid.htm

Made in the USA
San Bernardino, CA
15 January 2017